A PRIMER ON SCHOOL MENTAL HEALTH CONSULTATION

A Primer on
School Mental Health
Consultation

By

MORTON I. BERKOWITZ, M.D.

Clinical Assistant Professor in Child Psychiatry
School of Medicine
University of Pittsburgh

and

Senior Psychiatric Consultant
Allegheny Intermediate Unit
Pittsburgh, Pennsylvania

CHARLES C THOMAS · PUBLISHER
Springfield · Illinois · U.S.A.

Published and Distributed Throughout the World by

CHARLES C THOMAS · PUBLISHER

Bannerstone House

301–327 East Lawrence Avenue, Springfield, Illinois, U.S.A.

*With THOMAS BOOKS careful attention is given to all details of
manufacturing and design. It is the Publisher's desire to present books
that are satisfactory as to their physical qualities and artistic possibilities
and appropriate for their particular use. THOMAS BOOKS will be true
to those laws of quality that assure a good name and good will.*

This book was made possible by a grant
from the Maurice Falk Medical Fund.

Library of Congress Cataloging in Publication Data

Berkowitz, Morton I

A primer on school mental health consultation.

Includes index.

1. Child mental health. 2. School children—
Health and hygiene. 3. Student counselors.
I. Title. [DNLM: 1. Mental health services—In
infancy and childhood. 2. School health. WA352
B513p]

RJ111.B47   371.7′12   74–20697

ISBN 0–398–03342–0

Printed in the United States of America

K-8

To my daughters Janet, Lisa, and Ann through whose eyes I have been better able to see the world of the school child.

PREFACE

I FIRST LEFT the sanctuary of the child guidance center and private practice of child psychiatry in 1964 and ventured forth into the field of school mental health consultation. Prior to 1964 I felt that I was giving due recognition to the importance of school in the child's emotional problems and life experiences.

My involvement with schools at that time consisted of brief telephone conversations with teachers concerning impressions and recommendations around the child I was working with, occasional staff meetings with school personnel at the clinic or office, and a very rare visit to a school to discuss matters with a teacher and principal. Such was my involvement with schools until the history of a particular child was brought to my attention in November, 1963, which radically changed my entire approach to the role of schools in the mental health of our children. This child had been a thirteen-year-old boy who had been a chronic truant from school, disinterested in learning, and had manifested a very apathetic attitude toward school. He had been therefore referred to the local child guidance diagnostic facility for evaluation. At that time this is what one of the evaluators had to say about this boy:

> . . . a seriously detached, withdrawn youngster . . . a rather pleasant, appealing quality about this emotionally starved, affectionless youngster which grows as one speaks to him . . . no one [in his world] ever met any of his needs for love . . . [he] withdrew into a completely solitary and detached existence where he did as he wanted and he didn't have to live by any rules or come into contact with people. . . . [he] felt that his mother never gave a damn for him. He always felt like a burden that she simply just had to tolerate. . . .

Despite his withdrawal, he gives the impression that he is not so difficult to reach as he appears and patient, prolonged effort in a sustained relationship with one therapist might bring results. There are indications that he has suffered serious personality damage but if he can receive help quickly, this might be repaired to some extent.*

Whatever happened with this boy? Did he and his mother receive the help that was recommended for them? Unfortunately, as is often the case, due to a long waiting list and poor motivation on the mother's part, no help was ever received for this youngster. We may wonder, as with many other cases, whatever happened in this situation. In this particular case not only is there a follow-up on the eventual outcome, but the whole world was to learn of this boy. This youngster, who was diagnosed at age thirteen as emotionally disturbed and in need of help, was later to become the man who was to shoot and kill the President of the United States on November 22, 1963.

I began to wonder how many other potential Lee Harvey Oswalds were in our schools unrecognized or recognized as having emotional problems but nevertheless not getting the necessary help. This served as a sufficient catalyst to lure me away from the familiarity and security of the mental health environment and take a look at what was going on in the schools. This started in 1964 with a small grant from our local community mental health association.

It wasn't too long after I began to visit and attempt to consult in a public elementary school in a ghetto area that I discovered two very crucial factors. One was that the schools were very ill-equipped to help many disturbed students. The second was that I, as a child psychiatrist, was equally very ill-prepared to function as a helpful consultant. In the school I found teachers overwhelmed with large classes, disciplinary problems, rigid lesson plans, the obstacle of achievement tests, and conflict with administration. But it wasn't only the teachers who were overwhelmed. The same was true for many other school personnel. Principals were in a bind of being responsible for the school building and program and at the same time trying to be sup-

---

* Dr. Renatus Hartogs and Lucy Freeman, *The Two Assassins* (New York, Thomas Y. Crowell Company, 1965), p. 1.

portive to teachers. Guidance counselors, instead of really being able to counsel, were caught up with all kinds of administrative duties, questionnaires, and various forms. Social workers very often were not able to be more than glorified truant officers. School nurses, even though they often recognized that children were having emotional problems, in many cases were not able to do more than give a psychological Band-aid® to the hurt child. School psychologists were often desperately going around from school to school testing children and never quite testing all those who were referred and most often not being able to have meaningful dialogue with the child's teacher.

I began to get the impression that the child in need of some special help was helpless and caught up in a system that was helpless in providing what he needed and that I as a consultant was often helpless to provide meaningful consultation. The latter was primarily due to the fact that although I was a child psychiatrist, I had little training or preparation for working in schools and had very little knowledge of the peculiarities and problems inherent in large school systems.

In spite of this unfortunate situation I became exceedingly challenged to further school mental health consultation with the recognition that successful consultation could have very pragmatic and meaningful impacts on the emotional and educational life of our children. From that small beginning as consultant in 1964 in a single elementary school, I began to expand my time and energies to directing a mental health team in a socially disadvantaged area encompassing consultation to six elementary schools. I later switched my endeavors to our county school system, and we were to develop a consultation staff there consisting of psychiatrists, social workers, psychologists and paraprofessionals. A high point in our developing consultation programs in schools came in 1970 when our program was changed from mental health services to pupil personnel services, indicating recognition by the school board administration that mental health concerns are not external to school services but a natural part of pupil personnel services. My own personal evolution as a consultant has gone on to other levels, including a director of a mental health team, a director of a three-year federally funded demonstration project on school mental health consultation, a director of pupil personnel services in our county school system, and at present a senior psychiatric consultant to the Allegheny Intermediate Unit, a regional education service agency working with forty-six suburban school districts outside the city of Pittsburgh.

It is now ten years since I first began a timid consultation in the schools. I must admit that, because of the many problems in school consultation, I almost retreated back to the office and clinic. I am very glad that I did not. I am now more than ever challenged, stimulated, and impressed with the great value that *effective* consultation can have for the learning child, his teachers, his parents, and his therapist. This book is an attempt to share the hard earned and "battle scarred" trial and error experiences with you. It is not another attempt to describe still another school consultation program. It is certainly not intended in any way to be any kind of overwhelming textbook on school mental health. For this reason, you will note that there are very few references to the literature in this field. This book is an attempt to give a succinct "how to do it" approach to school consultation so that the reader can get some idea of this process in an expedient and nonthreatening manner.

I have often heard it said that school mental health consultation does not work, or has very little value. I feel this is said when a consultation has not been meaningful and helpful. I hope that what is to follow will provide an approach that can be helpful with demonstrating that, when handled in a sensitive way, consultation can be successful. This has particular relevance today to those in the mental health field who are more and more interested in doing school consultation, especially consultants who are working from consultation and education in the community mental health centers, consultants from clinics and child guidance centers, and individual consultants from the fields of psychiatry, psychology and social work. On the other hand, with the increasing use of the modality of school mental consultation, this book has relevance to all those working in schools who would be involved in the consultation itself, including teachers, administrators, guidance counselors, and nurses.

In closing, I'm reminded of an experience that occurred early in my consultation endeavors. I was asked by the teacher and principal to see an elementary school student who was having many behavioral problems. I had done so without obtaining parental consent. The following day, his mother angrily stormed in demanding to know "What is all this menthol health jazz about?" The following pages are an attempt to answer that question.

ACKNOWLEDGMENTS

THIS PRIMER was written while I was very busily involved in private practice of child psychiatry, teaching, and as consultant to the schools. I don't feel that it could have been completed without the invaluable help and support of various people. I owe a great debt to the Maurice Falk Medical Fund and its President, Philip B. Hallen, who provided me with a grant to write this book. I am also very grateful to Robert Jordan, who not only wrote the introductory chapter of this book, but played a constant devil's advocate role as a school superintendent. I want to especially thank Barbara Sipler, who was instrumental in the writing of the first draft of this manuscript with her suggestions and writing expertise. The manuscript itself was reviewed by several colleagues from different disciplines and their suggestions were extremely helpful. I, therefore, would like to thank Louis Charles, Ph.D. (Psychologist), Sondra Goldstein, Ph.D. (Psychologist), Edward Slagle, M.D. (Psychiatrist), Dorothy Reinhart, M.S.W. (Social Worker), and Phyllis Berkovitz (Teacher). In addition, I owe a great debt to my wife, Gloria, who was of constant support through many frustrating moments. Last, I would like to thank the very many school professionals who through their interest and candor, have enabled me to gain the insights that are shared in this book.

M.I.B.

Publication of this book was made possible by a grant from the Maurice Falk Medical Fund. The Fund, however, is not the author, publisher, or proprietor of the material presented here and is not to be understood, by virtue of its grant, as endorsing any statement made or expressed herein.

CONTENTS

A PRIMER ON SCHOOL MENTAL HEALTH
CONSULTATION

CHAPTER 1

A SCHOOL ADMINISTRATOR LOOKS AT MENTAL HEALTH CONSULTATION

THE SCHOOL ADMINISTRATOR FACES a constant tug of war: He is expected to carry out the mandate of the school board to reflect feelings and pressures of the community, and at the same time in his role as a professional educator, he wants to provide a quality education for as many children as possible. This tug of war is the major conflict repeatedly voiced by administrators in consultation.

It seems the administrator is always at a crossroads in dealing with the priorities of expending money, allocating time and directing attention. The educational program keeps going although the priorities become a little confused.

There are the public pressure groups, unions, deficits, and whims of school board members. All with the result of less and less time for the program of education for children. The public reads about the pressure groups in the newspapers. These groups may be the loudest, but seldom effect any real improvement in educational experience. The noise usually is about a changed bus route, coaching changes, or taxes. This may be important to the public but has little to do with significant educational improvement for large numbers of children.

It becomes very evident that the major thrust of the superintendent's job, and to a lesser extent that of other administrators in the system, is to maintain the system, to keep the schools going and, literally, to move from one crisis to another.

School administrators across the country encounter this situa-

Written by Robert Jordan, Former Superintendent, Avonworth School District, Ben Avon, Pennsylvania, and Assistant Professor, Business and Administration, Grove City College, Grove City, Pennsylvania.

3

tion, and interestingly enough, the typical superintendent today walks into the top school post not totally prepared for this tug of war. If you look at the typical superintendent, you'll find he entered the education profession as a teacher after a four-year training program and a degree in education.

Most superintendents have followed the same career pattern as mine. Teaching and working with kids was very satisfying, but the salary was not. After the first few years, economic needs began to become apparent—marriage, a family, and graduate school costs. The job of principal began to look good with its higher salary. Although I disliked leaving classroom teaching, I reasoned that I would still be working with kids and teachers.

After a few years as a principal, I was elected to the superintendency. My reasoning was that I could now influence the school board and the community to implement the good educational ideas that had been tossed around for years in the faculty room and in committee meetings, e.g. smaller classes, better equipment, special classes for exceptional kids, more guidance, more psychological testing, and better salaries.

As a new superintendent I made a good start. However, the problem of priorities became apparent. And to add to this constant struggle, the superintendent's job was further complicated by the sociological phenomena in today's society: instant communication, computer technology, protests, riots, black freedom, and working mothers. These factors all have a bearing on how kids are educated or at least how they are managed by the schools.

Everyone today seems to say, "I want to be me," or "I want to do my own thing." How does education work with all these "I's"?

As a former teacher, I was still *child-oriented*. Therefore, I knew I had to take a look at how the system within its almost necessary framework could be more responsive to the needs of all children. Was the so-called average child, the superior child, or the exceptional child getting the kind of education that would enable him to use his talents? Were mass teaching techniques really reaching enough of these children? Were there new and better ways to reach individuals according to their present needs and not mythical future ones?

As the superintendent I wanted to begin to effect change in the system. How would I begin?

First, I would have to recognize that my training as a teacher, typical of most teachers, had not really taught me to understand and teach the individual. Instead, all the techniques and methods I knew had to do with teaching classes and pointing my teaching to the average level of intelligence of those classes. This meant extra work for the brightest or extra time for the slowest, but I still taught to the academic level, now called the cognitive. There was rarely, if ever, enough concern with the affective or emotional level of children.

As an administrator I found that the problems with children faced by teachers and principals, although seemingly academic, often were in the emotional areas and with many causes. To deal with these children more effectively, a retraining in techniques, methods, and in attitudes seemed necessary. And this continues to be true. Unless the training of teachers has changed, and my close affiliation with training institutions says that it has not, teachers and administrators now in the system and teachers new to the system need some kind of retreading or retraining while on the job. This is a long, difficult job, but absolutely necessary if the needs of students for tomorrow's world are going to be better met by the educational system. If the system is going to better adapt to individual needs of students, then it is obvious that in-service training of teachers and other school personnel must take a different form than the conventional workshop and educational speeches of the past.

As the superintendent, I was continually seeking ways to reach all children, particularly those with problems. I was ready for suggestions, ideas other than we had in the system. We had problems that went on year after year with children and teachers that were not being solved under the present psychological assistance and family and child guidance clinics with their long waiting lists.

A number of times I had attended mental health conferences, always disappointed because talk centered on treating children clinically on a one-to-one basis. This was far from the classroom teacher's job of handling problem children within a classroom full of children. However, at one conference sponsored by the county health department, I heard something different. Both educators and mental health workers were talking together about models for collaboration between each discipline to help children with problems by pooling professional skills. Our district had worked with psychologists for years. In all fairness I must say that contacts with the psychologists, psychiatrists, and social workers as they worked with children were helpful, but their work indicated to me that they did not understand the classroom problem of a teacher trying to manage thirty to thirty-five children, some of whom had emotional problems. The fact is that they diagnosed, recommended, and walked away. The recommendation usually suggested that the teacher give the child more time and attention, and to an already overworked teacher, this was not much help. This was the standard consultant-teacher relationship.

However, at this particular conference there was talk about planning and working together to help children with problems. This sounded like a team approach to teaching with the focus on the child. In this type of collaborative program, the mental health worker would serve as a consultant for in-service training, working with teachers' attitudes rather than being looked upon as some sort of miracle worker to solve crises.

Standard practice in schools has been to call in the school psychologist when a child cannot be handled in the classroom. The psychologist is expected to test the child and tell the school what to do. At the conference schools were being asked to change their thinking. They were being asked to accept a mental health specialist from outside the school system to serve as a member of a team that would deal primarily with in-service training and consultation.

Not too long after that conference, our district was invited to participate in a federally-supported mental health program for seven districts which would put emphasis on attitude change of classroom teachers, so that they would better understand how to manage and teach the disturbed child within the classroom setting.* The program was part of the comprehensive pupil person-

* Reference is to the Title III ESEA West Central Pupil Personnel Project, Allegheny County Schools, Pittsburgh, Pennsylvania (1967–1970).

nel services of the county superintendent's office. We accepted the invitation to participate, but with some caution and trepidation.

In this seminar type of program, the participating teachers gathered information on children in the classroom and then collaborated with other members of a pupil personnel team including the guidance counselor, school nurse, psychologist, and social worker. Input about the child was given by each member of the team with the result that many concrete practical suggestions were made, which incidentally gave great moral support to the teacher with the problem child. The main goal was to broaden the teacher's way of looking at a student and thus help the learning child.

Districts participating in this program were committed to releasing several teachers for a half day, five days a week. Strong teachers were selected for the program even though at first glance many administrators felt the program would help the weakest teachers the most: those teachers who couldn't handle problems in the classroom and the teachers that bother administrators the most. The need for strong teachers on the team was explained in terms of the need to sell the program as it went along. More children could be helped by the more effective teachers. In addition, to introduce a new program such as mental health consultation, which is precarious to begin with, you have more of a fighting chance for a successful collaboration with the strongest people on your team.

Not only did the teachers need to accept the program, but also the principals, parents, and the school board. The principals were asked to release the teachers. Parents were asked to accept substitute teachers during the daily release time, and the school board was asked to accept the entire program. The release time for teachers was absolutely necessary, and the fact that federal funds almost completely covered this cost helped sell the program. It was necessary to take the teachers away from the classroom part of the time and then return them to the classroom to explore or practice what they had discussed in seminar sessions. This type of in-service training could not have been as effective without release time, and it was too big for an after-school program.

As the program developed, elementary and secondary principals and other specialists were involved in the collaboration along with the mental health workers from outside the educational field. In many cases the superintendents were reluctant to involve the principals in this type of program. It took them away from housekeeping or administrative chores. Then, too, the top man didn't want the principals involved right away until they saw that the program had value and until they were less threatened by it.

So the mental health workers sat back waiting. They knew that the principals were the bait needed to get mileage from the program. Theoretically, the principal is the educational leader charged with developing a program of instruction for children. His greatest obstacle, however, often is problem children. He is stymied; he doesn't know what to do with them. The conventional approaches—talking with parents, talking with psychologists, testing—are used, but the problem becomes the principal's because the teacher doesn't know what to do and routes the problems to the principal.

When the principals learned about the new program, they recognized that it might be an opportunity to do something for these troublesome kids. Something they had never been able to do before. In addition, the thought that the program would help them run a better program of education helped to get them involved.

Throughout this team approach in helping children with problems, the administrator was the enabler. He made released time for teachers possible. He encouraged his principals and his counselors, home and school visitors, and nurses to get involved, to take time from their busy schedules, and to attend the seminars. He got involved more directly himself, by brief oral or written reports on the successes and problems of the seminar. He supported and encouraged the program by dropping in on the sessions as an observer and sometimes a participant, but never as the dominant figure. And by being close to the program, the administrator assured the participants that they had his support. He showed this support by keeping the school board informed without scaring them, by answering inquiries from parents, other staff members and "those against any change." He became a positive and firm supporter.

As the program continued to grow, offshoots included seminars for superintendents as well as for principals at the secondary level. It was doubly important to have these administrators involved. If the program was to have any lasting effect or continuance after federal funds were phased out, the top administrators had to be involved.

As the program developed, mutual collaboration became the atmosphere in which professionals from several disciplines worked as a team to help a child by helping his teacher. As communication improved among team members, attitudes changed and children were helped. The team had within itself the necessary skills to try to solve almost any management or behavior problem with a chance of success.

Teachers began to change their attitudes toward problem children and to look for the cause of the problem. Along with the help of the team, they began to systematically analyze the facts gleaned from information about the child and his family, to seek assistance, and to try out agreed upon techniques for management of the child. Parents became aware of the great effort being made by the school to help their child, and they, too, became more knowledgeable and involved. Best of all, however, the child began to *feel* better mostly because he was now having some success in school and people cared.

Probably, however, the greatest gain was to the teacher herself, in the way her attitude often changed as she looked at all her children and their problems. This change in teacher attitude was extremely important from the administrator's viewpoint. In actuality, the administrators were looking to change some of the negative attitudes of teachers through this type of consultation, and the mental health consultants were aware of this wish. The system itself creates one of the greatest attitude problems: Large numbers of children in a classroom force teachers into the mold of being frustrated in time, materials, and accomplishments. And as a general rule, it is those kids who can't keep up who are unable to get more of the teacher's time.

Most of all the administrators wanted to encourage the attitude that every human being is worthwhile. We can't send the children back—they're the children of all the schools. Many times we know that some children may not be ready for learning a particular thing, but there are other ways. What other help can we get?

Many times it's the teacher's attitude. It's the way the teacher is oriented from her own training program. This orientation is to teach a mass of children, and the first fear is discipline, particularly when the students are older. When they're younger, the question is, "How can I keep them all busy doing something?" There is a technique; teaching doesn't come naturally.

Again, in all fairness, I have to say that teachers generally have feelings about kids as human beings, but they often don't know how to work with a mass of children. Their problem is how to do it when they're involved with a number of children. They don't know what to do, and the how and the what go together.

In addition, many teachers have the attitude that the child should be ready for their class, and if he isn't, he shouldn't be there. "It's not my fault," the teacher says, "and I shouldn't have to pick up the pieces. That is the previous teacher's job; that's the guidance counselor's job, or that's the psychologist's job—I've been trained to teach normal children."

Although the scene is changing, you have to remember that most teachers in the classroom today came from moderate middle-class homes. They really don't know much about distraught homes or mixed-up kids. They say, "Why should I have to deal with this type of kid? I came to a suburban district. I'm not supposed to have kids like that in my classroom." This is not an isolated attitude.

Mental health consultation did bring about changes in attitude. The type of approach in this mental health project was the most effective I've ever seen in schools. And with the changes in attitude, some children with no success stories started to chalk up positive records, and the teacher took a fresh look at the child. Of course, the case conference research helped teachers to better understand the child and his family, and some of this understanding got through to the parents who were better able to see their child in talking to the teacher.

Superintendents' attitudes also changed. At first my particular concern was that the consultation program did not fall flat on its face. The wrong handling of a parent by a teacher could bring the parent before the board, and it takes only that small action to kill a program with board members. Particularly a program in mental health which, as I said before, is a little shaky to begin with in a school system. Gradually, I became more and more sold on the project and most interestingly, I began to realize that the training and background of the mental health consultant gave him a considerably different outlook on children than the training and background of educators. In seminars educators and mental health consultants would pool their viewpoints, and many times I watched my staff members, many of whom I knew very well, perk up, get a look in their eyes, and then say, "Gee, I never thought of it *that* way." There is more than one way of looking at the child, and participants began to think a little differently, and attitudes began to change. The school grapevine started to put out affirmative information about teacher involvement and other staff members wanted to know more. Good news in the form of help for teachers spreads fast.

Of course, this consultation program is one model for a team approach to helping children and teachers learn more effectively. Obviously there are others. New curriculum programs in education place more responsibility for learning on the individual. Individually Prescribed Instruction, Independent Study, Process and Inquiry methods of teaching, all require a change of attitude on the part of administrators and teachers because they all require that the individual student be able to cope with his own problems first.

Whatever the model, it must include a kind of in-service training with practical help from specialists. The training must be done while on the job; I don't think it can be applied at the college level. When students come out of college, they are young and really immature in so many ways, mostly in terms of what children are like and what parents are like. Teacher training institutions place emphasis on content, educational theory, materials and methodology, and very little on the individual child and his problems. It would seem that in-service must be done after the teacher gets out on the job and has to deal with some of the emotional problems of children.

For too long the educational system has dealt with the cognitive side of the child only, and given lip service or blamed others for the child's affective or emotional problems. Good teachers and their administrators know that you can't separate the cognitive from the affective, because if the child can't learn, the system has to find out why and adapt, which means change. The students with problems no longer can be squeezed out of the system.

At last the priority seems to be on children, where it belongs, and probably mostly on individual children and their problems. Perhaps it includes a restudy of the educators' attitudes toward teaching, techniques, methods, and curriculum. At any rate, I have found that school mental health consultation, as I have experienced it, has helped greatly with positive modification of teacher attitudes and with the promotion of insight into the student's emotional self. As a school administrator I feel that this is the matrix for the success of any present or future teaching techniques in today's technological culture.

CHAPTER 2

SCHOOL MENTAL HEALTH CONSULTATION—WHAT'S IT ALL ABOUT?

WHY DO SCHOOL MENTAL HEALTH CONSULTATION?

THE NEED FOR CONSULTATION in the school has become increasingly apparent during the past few years as evidenced by the rise in school-related problems. Educators are well aware of such problems as student unrest, truancy, dropping out, and reading disabilities. (About 25% of today's students are reading below grade level.)

Mental health statistics (from the Report of the Joint Commission on the Mental Health of Children) show about four million school-age children in need of some form of professional mental health support, and statistics further point out that only 8.5 percent, or less than 500,000, are receiving help. Most of the children who are getting help, and all of the alarmingly high percentage who are not, attend our schools five days a week. These are our walking wounded; they are neither healthy enough to derive the maximum benefits from the learning environment nor disturbed enough to be removed from it.

In addition to the marked demand for increased mental health services in this country, there is a dire lack of the manpower necessary to meet this demand. It is quite obvious that there will never be enough therapists for these children. This is one reason why more and more therapists are converting some of their therapeutic time to serve as school consultants, thus extending their services in an attempt to help more children.

But the answer does not lie in remediation and therapy. It lies in the area of *prevention*. The need to explore models for prevention is graphically described by Gerald Caplan:

A telling model of the need for prevention is embodied in an old Cornish custom which was at the same time a simple and valid test of what might be called social insanity. In the 1600's a person suspected of being insane was put in a small room in front of a sink in which was placed a bucket. The faucet was then turned on. The subject was given a ladle and asked to empty the water from the bucket. If he tried desperately to bail the water out of the bucket without curtailing or attempting to reduce the flow at its source, he was considered insane. Any society or community which attempts in this twentieth century to provide bigger and better buckets of cure for behavior disorders without at the same time trying to reduce or stop the flow of their sources is equally suspect of insanity. I urge all of us to examine the tap, and to look for the tools and methods by which we can begin to turn it down or turn it off.

School mental health consultation endeavors to prevent disorders by providing methods for dealing with the source of the problem and not frantically suggesting buckets of cure *ad infinitum.*

The great need for mental health services for children in this country is obvious and the lack of enough therapists to meet this need is apparent. School mental health consultation is becoming a way to meet this problem of supply versus demand and the reason is two-fold.

First of all, as children spend more and more time in school, it becomes evident that mental health and learning are not separate entities. Good mental health is an essential and intrinsic part of the learning capacity of a child. Learning requires the necessary ingredients of inner freedom and peace of mind, motivation and maturity, as well as the opportunity to learn. This is in addition to the biological and physical factors also necessary for learning. Is it not true that these very same ingredients are also necessary for good mental health? How many times have conscientious teachers tried to reach children who, in spite of their intellectual ability, were not learning because they lacked sufficient motivation: They were depressed; they daydreamed; they were hyperactive? Whether these are considered mental health factors or educational factors is of no importance. That these factors are an essential part of the child's ability to learn —of his *educability*—is of utmost importance.

The second reason for school mental health consultation is that school is where the action is, and educators and mental health people can work together to help the learning child. The school is the best place for a variety of reasons.

School is Often Where Problems First Become Apparent

Most children seen by mental health professionals, whether in the private office, the clinic, or the hospital, have some form of school-related problem, either academic, behavioral, or both. For instance, symptoms of truancy, a sudden drop in grades, classroom misbehavior, and vandalism may be the first signs of emotional disturbance. Thus, the schools provide a natural vehicle for early identification of emotional problems and an opportunity primarily for prevention and secondarily for remediation.

School Has a Strong Influence on the Child

Mental health professionals have found that children with emotional and behavioral disorders very often lack self-confidence, self-reliance, and self-esteem. Most educators are well aware of the tremendous role the school plays in promoting these self-attitudes and capacities in the learning child. Schools can provide the climate to foster the growth of positive and sound self-images. When a child comes home from school at the end of the day, happy or sad, ask any parent if school has any influence on the way the child feels about himself.

School is Where Children Are Five Days a Week

Children are accessible to help without the necessity of depending on parents who might be unwilling or unable to obtain this help on their own. In many instances children from the hard-core, multiple-problem families are those most in need of help and those whose parents are unable to obtain help for them. Furthermore, in a majority of cases in which a child's school problem is identified as emotional in origin and referral is made to a psychiatric facility, this referral is either not accepted by the parents or is not followed through to the point of therapeutic effectiveness.

A school study in the Pittsburgh area showed that only 13

percent of the children evaluated and identified in school as needing some form of psychiatric help ever actually received this help. This statistic is not very different from attempts to refer school children for help in other areas of the country. Another study in a Pittsburgh child guidance center revealed that only 17 percent of the school children referred for therapy ever received it.

School is Where Trained Professionals Are Five Days a Week

Another argument for the suitability of the schools for mental health consultation is that it is the one place in a child's experience where, at a relatively early age, he is accessible to conscientious and interested professionals such as his teachers. When a youngster sets off for school in kindergarten or first grade, in many cases it is the first time in his development that he comes under the close scrutiny of objective professionals.

In addition, and this is of utmost importance in view of the manpower shortage in the mental health field, one does not have to bring in an army of professionals to help the child. They are already in the school building in the form of teachers, administrators, guidance counselors, nurses, speech therapists, and physicians. It makes sense then to capitalize on the existence of both a natural medium and professionals already on the scene to attempt preventive and early remedial measures.

WHAT IS SCHOOL MENTAL HEALTH CONSULTATION?

Having ascertained that school provides the common ground for the concern of educators and mental health workers for prevention and help, the next step is to define school mental health consultation. It may be stated as a *collaboration between educator and mental health consultant to help the learning child*. Parts of this definition bear emphasis and underscoring.

Collaboration means the process of the educator and consultant *actively* working together, not one party actively providing a service to a passive recipient. If the collaboration is successful, it will eventually eliminate the need for the consultant.

In this definition the *learning child* means that schools are for learning and not for transformation into mental health clinics or diagnostic or therapeutic institutions which make therapists of teachers. It is imperative that schools remain just what they were established to be—institutions of learning. A confusion of roles can be quite harmful and undermining. I have seen competent teachers lose confidence in themselves and even do harm to students when they were erroneously led to function as therapists.

Another aspect of the learning child in this definition focuses on the *total* child, including not only the cognitive but also the emotional aspects of learning, such as feelings, curiosity, self-concept, initiative, and autonomy. This interest in the learning child as the total child and not just an interest in helping a child to learn is again of concern to both the mental health professional and the educator.

Ekstein and Motto, recognized authorities in teacher training education, point out that teachers know that for the learning process to go, hopefully, from learning *for* love (of teacher) to love *of* learning there must be a healthy and positive identification with the teacher and learning. This very same identification is of interest to the consultant as a precursor to the child's becoming a healthy adult. The independence and self-reliance that the teacher tries to stimulate is the same as the freedom that the consultant seeks in order for the child to have the aggression required for looking, seeing, and hearing without being inhibited by anxieties and fears.

The things that teachers get excited about—interest, curiosity, creativity—make for a better student. Mental health people are just as interested in these factors because they know that these are the prerequisites to a healthy adult life.

WHERE SHOULD SCHOOL MENTAL HEALTH CONSULTATION TAKE PLACE?

There is little uncertainty about the choice of school as the setting for mental health consultation. The school is where the child spends a good part of his day, and it is part of his normal environment. Environment is part of the total child concept. Successful consultation cannot take place unless one has sufficient working knowledge of this environment. The only experience that many adults, including mental health workers, have in the classroom is their own childhood experiences as students.

Furthermore, it appears that once we are adults and out of school, we forget what it is like to be a child in school. If you don't believe it, spend a day in school experiencing the routine, the class climate, and the regimentation. It may surprise you how remote and distant you have become from the child's world.

In essence, the mental health worker is not merely trying to help a teacher understand what is wrong with a youngster, but also what is wrong with that youngster *in school*. To function knowledgeably, the consultant needs more than proficiency in child development and psychology. He needs an awareness of the child's school environment—his relationship with his teacher and his classmates, and his mechanisms for coping with school policies and expectations.

This kind of working knowledge is very difficult to obtain unless the consultant is willing to spend time in the classroom and the school, using the school as a site for the consultation process. The old model of having the educators attend a staff conference at a child guidance center as the means for providing consultation around the child is of limited value. How much more meaningful it can be for both consultant and consultee if they pool their understanding not only of the child but also of his school environment.

WHEN SHOULD SCHOOL MENTAL HEALTH CONSULTATION BE DONE?

A good axiom for the timing of consultation is *the sooner the better*. There has been sufficient experience to know, and studies indicate, that many school problems are detected and identified in kindergarten or first grade. Ideally, that would be the time for intervention. How often have we heard about the sixth grade youngster who now has a reading problem, is overly aggressive, doesn't complete his work, or is disruptive, only to find in going back through his records that this child was having difficulties in kindergarten or first grade. What is also of significance is that not only do almost all school problems have origins early in a child's educational career, but also that, without any outside professional help, the teacher is usually able to identify the problem. There are various programs, such as Head Start and others, that have already recognized this fact and have attempted to do something about it at the preschool level, realizing that the earlier the intervention, the better the prognosis.

WHO CAN DO SCHOOL MENTAL HEALTH CONSULTATION?

In the consultation process I am talking about a collaboration between educators and mental health consultants. One might ask specifically who shall be these collaborators? The mental health consultant or collaborator can be drawn from any of several disciplines, be it psychiatry, psychology, or social work. His effectiveness depends on his understanding of child development, of the school environment and of the interaction between both. In the most successful school consultation projects it should be difficult to determine the psychiatrist from the social worker or from the psychologist. This often would be a sign of an effective mental health team pooling their individual skills.

The educator-collaborator or consultee can also represent one of many different disciplines. Thus, an important decision for the consultant is with whom to work; an important decision for the school is the determination of the consultant's collaborator. The collaborator or consultee from the school can be from any level of the educational hierarchy, including the school board, administrators, principals, teachers, and pupil personnel workers (nurses, guidance counselors, home-school visitors, social workers). It might include direct work with the school child himself—although that becomes direct service rather than consultation—or some form of collaboration with the child's parents.

No matter who is designated as the consultee, *it is essential that both the consultant and consultee have administrative support.* A number of school mental health consultation programs have failed because there was insufficient support from the school board, the school superintendent, and/or the school principal.

The individual who is eventually assigned the role of consultee will depend on many factors which will be described in subsequent chapters. At this point we might explore briefly why one might state that any level in a school hierarchy can lend itself to productive consultation.

A consultant and school board might work together, focusing on the school as a social system seeing how such factors as discipline problems, personnel problems, and curriculum might affect the learning child. On the other hand, the school administrators, such as the school superintendent and his associates, might function as the consultees, working around such areas as class size, interviewing of teachers, academic grouping, establishment of classes for emotionally and socially disturbed children, aspects of curriculum, and many others.

Often it is the principal who could serve as the suitable collaborator. It is well known that the principal sets the tone and climate in his school, and this might be the target area for consultation. Discussion could concern itself with discipline, classroom practices, policy within the school building, teacher practices, and the intangibles that make up the general school atmosphere.

Another source for collaboration might be the pupil personnel worker, who in many ways is the school's internal mental health worker. It might be the guidance counselor to whom the problem youngsters are referred, or it might be the school nurse. She very often provides not only a first aid room for dispensing Band-Aids®, but also a mental health first aid room where many children come with their stomachaches, headaches, and other physical complaints arising from nonphysical and emotional reasons. Thus the mental health professional, together with the pupil personnel worker, might decide to collaborate and enable the pupil personnel worker to function more effectively in her job.

On the other hand, the mental health consultant might choose instead to work directly with the classroom teacher. I must stipulate here that in order to help the learning child in school —and this is the recommended goal for consultation—*one must collaborate directly or indirectly with the key person in his school life, his teacher.* In many ways the mental health consultant and supportive school personnel, including administrators and pupil personnel workers, are a form of teacher aides. The consultant can work at any level, but everything must filter down and be delivered through all levels in order for it to be used by the teacher in the classroom. Analogously, intelligence and supplies must filter down from top echelons to the men on the front lines in order for them to perform well in battle!

For many reasons, the consultant might not choose to or be able to collaborate directly with the teacher, but this does not detract from the fact that the consultation has to be of pragmatic value to the child's teacher. To recommend that a child receive more individual attention from a teacher struggling to cope with a class of forty children helps no one. But again I recommend that, where circumstances and climate permit, the consultant work with the classroom teacher.

Sometimes the consultee might be someone affecting school life but not serving as an integral part of the school, as for example, the child's parents. There have been various consultation programs where the main focus has been on the parents, with such activities as parent counseling and formation of parent groups.

Instead of the parents, sometimes community agencies, such as a boys' club, can affect the learning child and might become part of the consultation process and serve as the consultee.

Some consultation programs consult directly with the child himself, and this, too, can be a form of school mental health programming, but must be viewed more as direct service than as consultation. It bears repeating here that one of the chief benefits of a school mental health program is that it makes optimal use of mental health manpower which is in short supply. Direct service to children in school eliminates the advantages, to be detailed in later chapters, of consultation programs.

HOW DO YOU DO SCHOOL MENTAL HEALTH CONSULTATION?

Many times educators say they're in the school business not the mental health business, and yet both educators and mental health workers are concerned with the learning child. When the psychiatrist refers to symptoms, isn't this the same as the teacher's concerns and complaints? Many times the unmotivated child to the teacher is the depressed child to the psychiatrist. The day-dreaming child in the classroom often is the very same withdrawn and schizoid youngster in the psychiatrist's office.

The vital prerequisite for collaboration between educators and mental health workers is respect for each other's contributions with a capacity for learning to speak the same language and the ability to focus on the subject and reason for the consultation: the learning child. Focusing on any other aspect of the discipline by the consultant or by the consultee is irrelevant and often harmful unless it can be channeled to zero in on the learning child.

There are many built-in differences and conflicts between educators and mental health workers that can set up obstacles to this collaboration. Individual and personality differences exist as well as differences in training and methodology. Nevertheless, the important thing to remember is that the key word in school mental health consultation is collaboration. Future chapters will explore the steps to this goal and how to collaborate.

CHAPTER 3

RESISTANCES AND OBSTACLES TO THE CONSULTATION PROCESS

DESPITE THE importance of harmonious collaboration between the educator and mental health consultant to help the learning child, such harmony is difficult to achieve. Before a successful mental health consultation program can be conducted, many natural resistances built into the process must be overcome. It is therefore worthwhile to examine the collaboration from several aspects, to become aware of the obstacles in order to avoid them entirely, or handle them with greater understanding. The pitfalls may be within the area of the mental health consultant, within the school personnel, within the school system, or in the consultant-consultee relationship itself.

POTENTIAL PROBLEMS FOR THE MENTAL HEALTH CONSULTANT

LOCATION. For the consultant, the school he visits becomes a foreign territory which can become threatening and uncertain to him. Thus, as "a foreigner in a strange land" the consultant may not be aware of such important school customs as stopping by the office before he goes about his work or not detaining a child so that he misses the school bus.

ORIENTATION. Most consultants have been primarily trained to deal directly with an individual as in a doctor-patient relationship. Their background in community consultation is rarely extensive. They must therefore reorient themselves to the mode of group collaboration and consultation rather than to the one-to-one method of psychotherapy or casework. Thus recommendations that a consultant may give to a teacher that may be very applicable for the youngster they are talking about, may be totally

23

unfeasible and unrealistic in the group situation of a class of thirty to forty students.

CHILDHOOD EXPERIENCE. By and large the only experience a consultant has had with a school environment is his own as a child. To return to this atmosphere even though in a different capacity can awaken long dormant childhood fears, angers and prejudices and can produce a negative attitude toward the school, teachers or administrators. Several consultants on this basis automatically perceive the teachers and principals as "authoritarian bullies" and get off to a very bad start in attempting to establish a collaborative relationship.

BIAS. A consultant who has chosen to work in a field of child development and psychology tends to identify strongly with the child and is able to show great empathy for the child's limitations. This same empathy which is essential in helping a child can be a drawback if the consultant finds difficulty in also identifying with the limitations of the educator as a fellow human being. On the basis of such a preconceived bias the consultant may continually excuse and explain away the child's distressing behavior and make no allowances or provide no leeway for the teacher's limitations as a person. Sometimes consultants have to be reminded that not only children but also adults can hurt.

THE SYSTEM. The consultant frequently has insufficient knowledge of the school as part of a system. Therefore, recommendations he may make concerning a particular child, teacher, class or situation may not be applicable in a larger system. His advice to a teacher may be contrary to the principal's wishes or possibly not even be available in the school itself. I recall one consultant who based one of the main recommendations of his consultation on the child's having a quiet room where he could go when he felt overly pressured. It just so happened that in this very old school building which was already making use of every possible space for classes there was no such place as a quiet room.

TEAMWORK. The mental health consultant is often accustomed to adopting a directing role with patients and clients. It is often difficult for him to abandon this role and become part of the team because heretofore he has been captain of the ship. This may be harmful and interfere with an effective collaborative relationship. The consultant who directs in the relationship and *tells* people what to do may not be as successful as the consultant who *enables* people to do what might be recommended.

JARGON. The consultant may tend to make extensive use of psychoanalytic terms, e.g. oedipal conflict, symbiotic relationship, transference. Though there may be a need to understand these concepts in order to work more successfully with the problem child, the use of such terms can be a mistake. The consultant who uses these terms unnecessarily and excessively may be enhancing his own professional image but does so at the expense of also increasing the gap between himself and the consultee. A consultant should become concerned if the teacher is heard to say, "Well he may be very smart, but this has been of little help to me." The art is to think like a psychiatrist but not to sound like one.

POTENTIAL PROBLEMS FOR SCHOOL PERSONNEL

THE THREAT OF THE OUTSIDER. Frequently the consultant encounters resistance because he is an outsider encroaching on the teacher's territory. He may be perceived as a stranger coming in and "telling us how to run our school or to spy on us and find out our inadequacies." The teacher may be already sensitized from past experiences to anticipate criticisms. This preconditioning may make it difficult to view the consultant as a fellow collaborator rather than another kind of critical supervisor.

ROLE REVERSAL. The teacher is resistant to being placed once again in the role of student, being taught how to teach a problem child. The teacher, like the consultant, is accustomed to disseminating knowledge in her classroom. The role reversal in consultation where the teacher may see herself as a student once more can be threatening. This may be expressed as "what does he know about math" when the real issue is on the child who is to learn math.

ACADEMIC ORIENTATION. The teacher by training is geared to handle the academic problems of her students. The cognitive sphere may be much more familiar and comfortable than the affective sphere. Thus the teacher frequently prefers seeing the child's problem as an academic one rather than an emotional one.

For instance, the teacher may say, "He would not have any problems if he only did his work neater, if he only handed in his homework on time." This difficulty can cause resistance to attempt to become more aware of the emotional and affective life of the student.

INVOLVEMENT. Teachers may tend to resist involvement with their students in nonacademic ways if this may cause particular anticipatory anxiety. They may fear opening a Pandora's box of emotional problems of the students. The anticipated concern and apprehension is that if they were to get into the child's problems, it might be overwhelming. This concern is often expressed by teachers with such comments as, "What you don't know won't hurt you."

EXPECTATIONS. The teacher is often accustomed to spoon-feeding knowledge to her students. In turn, she may expect the consultant to spoon-feed answers to her problems. When she is unable to cope with a child, she looks for omniscience on the part of the expert. The more helpless she is in a situation, the more she looks to the consultant for all the answers. When he cannot give her all the answers, she may become pessimistic and discouraged about consultation. I have often seen teachers disillusioned that the consultant did not have the magic answer, and the consultant frustrated that this was expected of him.

SELF-ESTEEM. When a teacher seeks help for a child, she often suffers from a personal sense of failure. To be involved in consultation might seem as an acknowledgement of her inadequacies and could lead to defensiveness, guilt, and lessening of self-esteem. This can make a positive consultation relationship difficult. Many times the initial picture presented in a consultation problem was not "where the real problem was at." And it was only after the teacher felt less defensive that she could begin to look at what was really going on.

MYTH. Among school personnel there is a myth that the mental health worker is really evaluating the mental health of the school faculty. This can lead to distrust, loss of candor, fear and obstructionism. This kind of concern is heard through such sarcasms as, "Here comes Dr. Anthony to solve all our problems," or "Let's get out the straightjacket boys; here's the shrink."

POTENTIAL PROBLEMS FOR THE SCHOOL SYSTEM

Perhaps the easiest way to describe the resistance of the school system to the consultation process would be to use the analogy of the heart transplant. When a new and healthy heart is grafted on to the existing organism, the organism's natural rejection of any foreign body ultimately causes it to fail. The grafted organ is sound, but the body's natural defenses will ultimately reject it. Thus no matter how healthy the consultation process, the built-in resistance to the outside service (consultation) grafted on to the system may cause it to fail. I would like to point out some of the natural built-in defenses that are part of the school system itself.

THE AUTHORITARIAN HIERARCHY. A school system is hierarchical and authoritarian in structure. It does not readily lend itself to a working relationship or an active involvement with outside professionals. For example, a consultant may wish to work with a classroom teacher but he must first clear this with the principal, the hierarchical or vertical levels cannot be bypassed.

INTERDISCIPLINARY RIVALRY. In addition to hierarchical obstruction on the vertical level, there is another form of obstruction at a horizontal level. Rivalry exists on an interdisciplinary level as between teachers and guidance counselors, setting up a power struggle that impedes the creation of a unified base for consultation. The consultant may wish to work with the classroom teacher, for example, but the guidance counselor may feel this is his domain and thus knowingly or unknowingly undermine the relationship between the consultant and the teacher.

PROGRAM ORIENTATION. The system seems to be primarily program-oriented rather than child-oriented. There is concern over the operation of various aspects of running the system such as time lapse during class changes, or dismissal of all children at a certain time for buses. This may conflict with the needs of the student. For instance, a teacher cannot be available to a child who seeks her out because the school demands that she dismiss her class promptly.

THE THREAT OF EXPOSURE. Because the school is part of the child's environment, it is a necessary part of the examination of the child's difficulty. The school can and often does react with the same defenses as would an individual teacher by trying to hide the skeletons in the closet. A school district known to have many problems responded to the offer of consultation with the statement, "We are able to handle all our own problems, and any help should be in the form of giving us more teachers."

PRESSURES. Schools are under heavy pressure from both parents and from the community. Anxiety about this pressure may inhibit freedom to consult or to follow through with recommendations concerning the problem child. An example of this pressure in action would be the dress and grooming code. The consultant may recommend leaving the child alone and not responding negatively to his dress or hair length. This may not be feasible because community pressure for conformity may not allow the school to go along with this recommendation.

ISOLATION. Often a school is a society unto itself. And in many ways, it is isolated and fragmented from other child and youth facilities in the community, especially from mental health facilities. This can force the feeling of alienation that can create distance between consultant and consultee. This might be expressed as "you people over there at your place can do it that way, but over here, this is how we have to do it." The implication here is that over there might be a million miles away when in actuality, it might be just several blocks away.

CONFLICTS IN THE RELATIONSHIP ITSELF

GROUP VERSUS INDIVIDUAL ORIENTATION. Teachers are group-oriented since they spend their time in classroom situations. Psychological personnel, on the other hand, are individual-oriented since they have been essentially trained to deal on a one-to-one basis primarily trying to understand the dynamics of individual behavior. I have often heard a teacher say regarding a consultant's recommendation, "That would be great if Gary was the only kid in the class." The problem then, is to knit the group-oriented teacher and the individual-oriented mental health consultant together to function as a unit in the school setting.

ACTION VERSUS WAIT AND SEE. Teachers are geared to solutions involving immediate action. When a problem arises such as a child refusing to do his work or defying the teacher, some immediate response is called for. The mental health worker, how-ever, explores, investigates, and studies introspectively. His ad-vice to the teacher of "wait and see," is often unsatisfactory to the teacher who must face the situation in the classroom the fol-lowing morning. Therefore, the consultant must try to effect an accommodation between the two orientations. This problem may be expressed as "well, what you are recommending may work out very well three weeks from now; but what should I do tomorrow when I have to see this youngster at 10 A.M.?"

CONTROL AND MANAGEMENT VERSUS EVALUATION AND DIAG-NOSIS. The teacher in the classroom is concerned with various symptoms: inattention, incomplete work, and disruptive be-havior. She is seeking help in the management of these symptoms, which she verbalizes in her complaints about the child. The mental health specialist is less concerned with symptom manage-ment than he is with arriving at diagnosis. Once he has learned the cause he will try to treat the symptoms. This problem has been voiced, for instance, by one teacher who said, "If I have a very severe headache, I want something to relieve the pain, and not have to wait until the cause of the headache is determined." The management-oriented teacher and the diagnosis-oriented mental health specialist must adapt to each other in order to collaborate meaningfully.

DISPOSITION VERSUS RECOMMENDATION. A teacher in a classroom of thirty or forty pupils, when confronted by a child with learning difficulties, is often seeking some disposition for the problem youngster to alleviate the pressures of trying to teach too many children. The goal of the disposition may be to relieve the teacher rather than to help the child and may involve transfer to another class, suspension, or placement in a special education class. Thus, the problem is *disposed of*. The mental health con-sultant is primarily concerned with serving the needs of the child, and making diagnoses and recommendations before any dispo-sition is made. For example, his recommendation may be that a very passive, inhibited and withdrawn youngster remain in the classroom and measures be taken to help remove his inhibitions. This may be different from what the teacher hoped for with the disposition of putting the child in a slower learning class since his passivity prevented him from becoming sufficiently involved in his present classroom. It might be that the placement in a slower learning class might just allow more opportunity for the student to become more withdrawn. Thus this problem of disposition versus recommendation must be reconciled.

DISTURBING VERSUS DISTURBED. The teacher usually seeks help for the disturbing youngsters in her class. Often these children manifest aggressive behavior, disruptiveness, and other misbehaviors. On the other hand, the mental health consultant is interested not only in the disturbing child, but also in the disturbed one as well. *The child who is a problem is not necessarily the one who has a problem, and the most troublesome child may not be the most troubled child.* Thus, a very quiet, introverted, daydreaming child may not be disturbing to the teacher, and may not distress her, but he might well be of concern to the mental health consultant who might see this behavior as a sign of marked withdrawal and inner psychological distress. A conflict would then exist between the teacher and mental health consultant, both wanting to concentrate on very different aspects.

TEACHING VERSUS LEARNING. Through teacher training, and also under pressures of lesson plans, achievement tests, and material to be covered, the teacher is primarily concerned with the teaching process and what is being taught. The mental health specialist whose training directs his interests to growth and development is primarily interested in the learning process within the child rather than just the curriculum. Again the two approaches must be welded together to help the child in the classroom. The teacher at times has to be reminded that he teaches English to students and the mental health consultant at times has to be reminded that the student is there to learn English.

IQ VERSUS EDUCABILITY. Historically, a child's ability to learn has been perceived by educators to be based on his intellect and the cognitive aspects of learning. Learning is seen in terms of intelligence tests, performance on achievement tests, and demonstration of the acquisition of principles and concepts. The mental health consultant sees not only the child's intellect, but also the attitudinal and emotional factors in his learning process or his educability. Besides his intellect, the student's educability is based on his self-image, his feeling of adequacy, his ability to function independently, and his freedom to explore. In the mental health field, it is also the underlying feelings that are a prime concern and not only the overt acquisition of knowledge. Thus for example, the teacher may be wondering why Jimmy isn't learning because everyone knows he is such a bright boy. Whereas, the consultant may be wondering how Jimmy can learn when he is so anxious that everyone expects him to do far better than he feels he is able to.

DIRECT SERVICE VERSUS INDIRECT SERVICE. The teacher is service-oriented, seeking help for her concerns caused by the problem child. The consultant is trying to help the child by expanding the teacher's understanding of that child. Thus a teacher may line up five problem youngsters to be evaluated by the consultant while he arrives planning to meet with five teachers in order to help understand the children in their classes. In other words, the teacher may want a form of mental health clinic in the school complete with diagnosis and treatment, whereas the consultant would like to focus on the total school climate for both teachers and children.

UNILATERAL VERSUS BILATERAL ADAPTATION. When the teacher is not able to help a non-learning child and has exhausted all her own resources, she seeks consultation with the overt or covert wish for the mental health consultant to *cure* or *do something* with the child. In many cases, the consultant is not able to do either. He is just as interested in helping the teacher and the class to adapt to the youngster, as well as helping the child to adapt to the class, not just making the child fit the mold, but making the mold fit the child. The teacher may seek a unilateral adaptation of the child in school, or his removal from school should he fail, whereas the consultant may seek a bilateral adaptation of the school and teacher-classroom.

Obstacles vary from school to school and not every obstacle will be encountered in a given consultation program. The programs are as individual and varying as the schools and communities in which they exist and as the differences in the personnel involved. However, the obstacles can all be there to a greater or lesser degree. Awareness and sensitivity to these obstacles can make a difference in the success or failure of a school mental health consultation program. I must admit that many of these resistances and obstacles I only came to see in retrospect after many trial and error endeavors and mistakes. Sometimes, it was the pain of my own mistakes that led me to being aware of the roles some of these obstacles played, and other times it was honest and candid feedback from the consultee.

The following chapters will be devoted to making positive use of the awareness of these obstacles and trying to demonstrate how a mental health consultation program can be successfully and effectively implemented. The fact these difficulties do exist, but can be met, and the knowledge that school mental health programs can be successful has led to the writing of this primer.

approach. Of course, being a guest in a school can bring mutual doubts and insecurities to both the consultant guest and host school. The consultant may be unsure and anxious about the nature of his welcome and the length of his stay. On the other hand, the school may be anxious as to how to receive this guest and outsider.

Furthermore, a consultant serving a school system may be invited or uninvited. In the case of the invited guest it is analogous to the situation where the father invites a guest home to dinner. It is assumed that the rest of the family will accept the guest at that moment. The guest's behavior will determine his further acceptance or rejection by others in the family. A parallel situation exists in the school system. The administration may invite the consultant in as their guest; the risk, though, is that the school personnel might not accept the guest, depending on the manner in which he handles himself as well as their readiness to receive him.

The Invited Guest

The invitation can come from any source within the school system. Most often it comes from the administration who feels the need for some form of mental health consultation and is seeking advice from a local mental health facility or individual consultant.

Sometimes the initial stimulus comes from teachers. In one system, part of the negotiation package at the time of a teachers' strike was a request for mental health consultation. The teachers had previous consultation experience, found it helpful in the classroom, and wanted more of this kind of help.

At other times, parental pressure, for instance the PTA, can bring consultation into the schools. In one instance, a PTA stimulated the administration to obtain consultation services and then paid out of their own funds to bring in a psychiatrist to meet with the teachers one afternoon every two weeks.

Still another source can be the school board. In one case, the consultant had treated the son of the president of the school board in his private practice. The president recognized the value of this kind of knowledge of children and realized that it would be helpful to teachers. He then volunteered to light the fire under the school board members and school administrators and so a consultation program was launched.

In another case, the consultant wasn't invited by the school system, but the match was lit by a local community mental health agency that recognized the need for consultation in their local school system. They realized that the school system and mental health facility were quite far apart so they served as the intermediary to find the consultant and then tapped their own funds to pay him. All this was done with the hope that the success of the program would lead to a complete school-financed consultation program. The consultation proved to be a positive experience for both the school and consultant and from that interaction the entire consultation program evolved.

Entry can also be gained by private practice therapists or staff members of mental health facilities who are working as therapists with children in a particular neighborhood or school system. Their work will take them into contact with teachers and other school personnel concerning the children under their care. If the school system finds that mental health consultation enables them to help a problem child, there is a possibility that they might say, "How about coming in and helping us with some other children?"

Another experience that has permitted the invitation of the mental health consultant into schools has been the introduction of classes for emotionally disturbed children. In many states, in order to receive state subsidy for these classes, the state mandates a psychiatric and psychological screening of the students for these classes. Mental health workers therefore, have been invited into the school system to consult with these special classes, and in many cases, if the consultation has been favorable, it has been extended to other areas of the system.

The Uninvited Guest

What does a mental health worker do if he feels there is a need for this type of service in a school system even though the school might not recognize or want it? How does he get himself invited into the school or get a foot in the door?

Indirectly the consultant can actively campaign by speaking at

PTA meetings and mental health meetings known to be attended by school personnel. In many instances it is quite natural to speak on issues of common concern to both mental health people and the schools, e.g. juvenile delinquency, drugs, learning disabilities. This can provide an opportunity for exposure to school personnel and might lead to an invitation into the school system. In one instance, a psychologist gave a speech at a public meeting on drug abuse where concerned school administrators were in attendance. A consultation program is now in its third year at a large city high school as a result of this meeting.

The uninvited guest is becoming more of a problem today due to the fact that more and more mental health professionals aspire to reach children through school consultation. This is particularly true in the national network of community mental health centers which have a C and E function (consultation and education) with a major thrust directed toward school mental health consultation. This puts the mental health professional in a position of trying to get himself into the school system. He is seeking out the school, and often the school is not seeking him. One large center located in a well known hospital went to the schools with a message: "We have professionals who would like to help you; do you want their help?"

The best advice, however, is to go where you are wanted if at all possible. Experience has shown that the easiest way to enter the school system is as an invited guest, and even with an invitation, the consultant can encounter a great deal of built-in resistance at first. The consultant is almost looking for headaches if he goes where he hasn't been invited.

PHASE 2: PRELIMINARY EXPLORATION PRIOR TO SETTING UP A CONSULTATION CONTRACT

Now that the consultant has been able to gain entrance into the school, the question is: "Now that I'm there, what do I do next?" At this point the next phase of the process is a two-fold exploration. The first is to assess the needs of the school for a consultation program, and the second is to assess the manner in which the consultant can meet these needs. Actually this process is a mutual appraising of each other's need and abilities to meet them. It may be that what the school is asking of the consultant is unrealistic and not feasible. On the other hand, it may be that the consultant is not the proper person to meet a very real need of the school system. This process cannot be rushed. The resulting mutual understanding make the time and trouble worthwhile. In one case the mental health consultant spent an entire summer to achieve merely first stage accord with the administration. When school began in the fall, he proceeded with exploratory meetings with the faculty. Only when the contract was thus clarified could they actually begin consultation.

To achieve the essential rapport between consultant and consultee, certain prerequisite conditions must be met. Obviously, it is necessary to secure the administrative support, either from the superintendent or from the school principal. The next is to be welcomed by the faculty. For no matter how eager the administration is for your services, the consultant will often fail unless the faculty is equally receptive. It is therefore mandatory that the contract drawn by the administration and the consultant represent both the administration and teachers' needs and expectations. If the administrator is not backed by his faculty, the consultant would be ill-advised to enter into a contract unless faculty support is achieved. If the faculty has the attitude that "they can force mental health on us, but they can't make us like it," the program is most likely doomed from the start.

If the consultant explores the contract with the top administrators only, he will find that the requested help does not match the needs or desires of the grassroots personnel with whom he will be working.

In a city district, the administration asked two consultants, a social worker and psychiatrist, to work with six elementary schools in one geographic area. The administration told the grassroots personnel that consultation would be available to them and that was all that was said. They were never asked how they felt, how they wanted to use the consultants, or even if they wanted any consultation services at all.

As a result, each school expected something different. The first school envisioned a miniature mental health clinic in their own building with the two consultants seeing all the disturbed children, evaluating and treating them. The principal and teachers in the second school had group experience and pictured the consultants as group leaders, helping children through the technique of group therapy. The third school had no expectations or anticipations, realistic or unrealistic, about the consultation help. In fact, they felt it was administratively imposed on them simply because the school was in that geographical area. The consultant met tremendous resistance later as indicated by the principal's comment: "I am told that we have to work together, but I would like to know who's going to make it work." In the fourth school, where the belief was that most behavior problems could be corrected by strong discipline, the consultants were envisioned as the ones to provide techniques for whipping the kids into line. In the fifth school the staff was greatly distressed that consultant services were to be provided. This staff had many problem students and teacher morale was low. The teachers reacted to the offer of mental health consultation with a feeling that the consultants were there to work on them and "to straighten them out." The sixth school had still another reaction. Previous consultation experienced at this school had been favorable, and the teachers had been helped with problem youngsters. In fact, it was this principal who had asked the administration for more consultation services. The expectation of this faculty was to meet regularly with the consultant to better meet the needs of problem students. They didn't line up a bunch of kids for the consultant to treat; they lined themselves up for regular meetings with the consultant.

It is obvious that each group expected something different, but the most interesting aspect is that these expectations, except in the sixth school, were totally counter to the consultants' ideas and thoughts on the most helpful way to work with the teachers.

Of course, the reverse situation may develop. The mental health consultant gets the support of the teachers or others with whom he works, but then fails to get administrative support. For example, in a consultation session centering on a particular child, both the consultant and consultee felt that the child should take certain academic courses at a level he could handle even though they were below his grade level. This meant changes in curriculum policy. The administration vetoed the changes; it was against their policy. This decision, of course, led to mutual frustration for the teacher and consultant alike. A cardinal principle in school mental health consultation, therefore, is that the consultant must have an opportunity to explore needs and desires with the personnel with whom he is going to work.

To compound the problem, often there are unexpressed and covert needs in the picture that the consultant will not discover until later because he is not part of the school system, and it takes time to learn about these problems. For example, in a local school district, the expressed need was: "Yes, mental health is part of learning, and we would appreciate consultation to help us with the learning problems because we know the two go together." This need was expressed by the administration and was agreeable to the consultant.

Later, however, the consultant discovered an unexpressed covert expectation. Parents had been complaining to the school board that the teachers and principals were too punitive and there was far too much paddling and suspension. Through mental health consultation, the administration hoped to remove the punitive attitude; however, the consultant never heard this side of the story in the initial exploratory phase. The principals' group with whom the consultant was to work knew and resented the attitude of the administration, and as a result viewed the consultant as an axe man or tool of the administration. The consultant met with great resistance without understanding its reason until later on in the consultation experience.

One of the most common problems encountered by the consultant will be verbalized as asking the consultant for help with problem children. However, on the nonverbal level, the consultant is being asked to be an ally in one of the many internal power struggles going on in the school system. In a particular school district, the administrators and teachers asked for help. In actuality they were asking for an ally against the guidance counselors whom they felt were acting as if they were experts in dealing with students and sharing very little of their understanding with the teachers. There was a tremendous amount of antagonism and alienation between the guidance counselors and

unveiling expectations

the rest of the staff. The nonverbal desire came out very clearly after awhile, and the consultant felt as if he were being asked to pick sides.

On the other hand, it may be the consultant who is speaking out of both sides of his mouth. He, too, can be guilty of expressing verbalized agreement while remaining silent about his real feelings. He also can be criticized for expressing one idea and meaning another. If a consultant views a school as being too rigid, too inflexible, or too authoritarian, he might agree on the verbal level to help the teachers understand the children better; however, on the emotional level his attitude is to go in and soften up those rigid, inflexible teachers. He already is walking into the school with a chip on his shoulder, an attitude that will not help establish rapport.

PHASE 3: THE WRITING OF THE TYPE OF CONTRACT

After mutual exploration, which results in the feeling that the consultant and educators can collaborate to help the learning child, the next step is to define a contract on the method of working together. In general, two types of contracts can be considered here. The first is a trial or exploratory one in which certain kinds of things will be done on a trial basis. It is not any more definitive than trying an idea to see how it works. The second type is a more structured contract and is the definitive type that is more specific in its design.

One example of the trial contract might be where the guidance counselors are picked as the first group to work with the consultant. If this works well, teachers and principals might later become involved. The reason for choosing the guidance counselors could be that they are already more socially and psychologically oriented and might be the best people to positively launch the program.

In another type of trial contract, the wish might be to have the total faculty of a school building involved in a consultation program; however, there may be concern that several teachers will not be interested or motivated. Therefore, rather than choose the total faculty approach, the trial contract may be first tried with a group of motivated teachers with the hope that this will be successful and favorably influence the remaining staff. This is what has often been called *the ripple effect*.

In the second type of contract, the definitive contract, one specifies the consultant's approach and designates the consultee. For instance, a group of principals is to be the key consultation group in the school district. Consultation efforts will be directed toward this group. Once this specific contract is fulfilled, and the consultant feels the principals are actively involved in support of consultation, a move then can be made to work with other consultee groups such as the teachers.

Some school systems are more ready than others to try specific approaches, and there is less inclination to the trial type of contract. Therefore, the contract can be spelled out right away. In a school system that is already sold on the pupil personnel team approach (teachers, principals, guidance counselors, and nurses meeting with a consultant to discuss specific children), and where the consultant feels positive about this approach, there will be no trouble in making a definitive contract. Another school system, unfamiliar with this approach and not too sure of its merits, might set up a trial contract for this program.

Whichever type of contract is set up, it is important that there be a realistic assessment of the needs of the school and a determination of how well the consultant can professionally meet these needs. It must be mutually decided what is needed, and how much of it the consultant can provide. The consultant can suggest what he feels may be needed, but he can do only as much as the school personnel agree they need and want. A consultant attuned, for example, to sensitivity training should not force this technique on the school personnel if it is neither what they want nor feel they can handle.

By far, the most difficult of problems in setting up the contract, and one that is encountered time and time again, is the expectation of the school in wanting direct service and help for children with problems and the expectation of the consultant to provide in-service training programs, teacher attitude modification approaches, and other less direct service oriented approaches. In one district, the consultant found that the verbalized agreement was to help teachers better understand what the influences on children's feelings relevant to learning are. The non-verbalized component of the contract was the desire for the consultant to take care of the problem children and, by taking care of the children, the teachers meant *to cure them, or get rid of them.* This, of course, was not verbalized, but in consultation sessions it later became apparent in the teachers' attitudes.

On the other hand, the consultant can also be guilty of a non-verbal expectation. As much as the school wants to cure or oust its problem children, the consultant may feel as strongly that every child is teachable, even though certain children may be far too ill to be able to be reached in a regular classroom situation. Both expectations are unrealistic, and when neither one is really expressed, the consultant and consultee wind up at cross purposes. At its thorniest best, the consultant and the educators have a long way to go when the consultant seeks to introduce in-service training aimed at prevention, and the school wants nothing more than direct service to students. Since this is one of the major problems in collaboration, it will be discussed at different times subsequently.

CHAPTER **5**

SELECTING THE CONSULTATION MODEL

I N DRAWING UP A CONTRACT with a school system, the consultant can suggest different approaches, basing suggestions on his experience and the prior experience, or lack of it, of that particular school system. There are various models that can be considered in looking at the different types of consultation. The first major category in which different models of consultation can be found is in the general rubric of the school system itself. And here, specifically, one may address consultation to various aspects and components of the school system: namely, the students, the personnel involved in working with the students, and lastly, the school program itself. The second major area for models of consultation is where the particular model used is primarily focused at some level of prevention; the level of prevention determines the consultation model.

CONSULTATION BASED ON A SPECIFIC COMPONENT OF THE SCHOOL SYSTEM

Direct Consultation

Consultation Service to the Student

Consultation service to the student directly is actually more in the form of direct service rather than true consultation. Nevertheless, often as part of a broader consultation some direct service to students may be necessary to allow other models of consultation to be initiated. In general, direct consultation with students is either on an individual basis with a particular student, or on a group basis with a group of students.

One instance where many times direct consultation with an individual student is helpful is a kind of on the spot evaluation.

This often is requested when a youngster is presenting a very critical, pressing problem to the school. Rather than refer the student to a prolonged delay of receiving service at a local mental health facility, the school may ask the consultant to evaluate the child within the school system and try to answer some of their immediate concerns. In some cases the consultant meets with the student in order to advise the teacher how to cope with him. In other cases, different goals may be considered such as some other disposition for the child who is creating anxieties in the school. Many times this approach is more feasible because outside help is not as knowledgeable as consultation services that are within the school system and also as already mentioned, not as readily available. One example of this type of on-the-spot consultation was in a situation where a high school student suffered a psychotic breakdown in class. As a result of this, he was hospitalized at the local state hospital and after a sufficient course of improvement was discharged from the hospital and told to return to school. Not only was the school fearful of receiving the student after having experienced a frightening psychotic episode, but also the student was fearful of returning to the school where he had experienced considerable anxiety, embarrassment, and humiliation because of his bizarre behavior. At this point the mental health consultant was asked to evaluate the student and to work out a plan for his return. The hospital had provided no help in this regard beyond the statement that the student could return to school. The consultant met with the student, evaluated his situation and the school's situation, and from this a plan was devised where the student, who was not ready for the total classroom situation, could attend school during the latter part of the day to receive individual instruction from several of his teachers. As the teachers worked with the student in this gradual and nonthreatening situation, both teachers and student regained confidence and the student was eventually able to return to the classroom in about three weeks.

At other times, the need for direct involvement of the consultant with the student may be with a group of students rather than an individual student. This may center around various student problems: drug abuse, obesity, underachieving, or poor peer relationships. In this situation, the consultant would meet with the students to help them in their problematic areas. Sometimes, the consultant would meet with the students and serve as a group leader, and at other times, he may meet with a teacher or other school person as a co-leader. As the group begins to make progress, he may then bow out and allow the school person to continue as the group leader. He then may serve as a resource person for the group leader who is working directly with the students.

One example of this type of consultation model was a situation in which a third grade teacher took an interest in a group of five boys who were underachievers and had a very low opinion of themselves in regard to their own self-image and their scholastic achievement. The youngsters, although intellectually capable, were passive, poorly motivated, and lacked initiative. The teacher met with them twice a week for an hour, not to focus on their lack of confidence in school work but to stimulate them in areas in which they could be successful. The students designed and made props for a class play, raised money for the United Fund, and helped keep the classroom clean. In these tasks the boys were successful, which helped them to think better of themselves and to receive recognition from their classmates for their job. In fact, this group raised the greatest amount of money for the United Fund. This approach generated activity, decreased the boys' passivity, and spilled over into academic areas. The students became more involved in the learning process and received more respect from their classmates. This latter result helped to reinforce a more positive self-concept.

In another consultation at the high school level, a group of eight boys in the tenth grade were showing signs of becoming prospective dropouts through repeated truancies, cutting of classes, incomplete work assignments, and discipline problems. The boys lacked positive identification with themselves and with the school. An assistant football coach, a strong male identity figure, instituted group sessions with these boys, meeting with the group for two hours a week. Here, too, rather than focusing directly on their failures in school, the boys were encouraged to focus on any subject on which they had an opinion. In this case the main textbook used was any magazine that sparked the interest of the boys. They then were asked to discuss a personality or topic from their reading and to gather additional information from the library or field trips. The coach and his group attended athletic events together, and after the game, the group would discuss the game and the players. Interest was generated in the lives of famous athletes, and the students then wrote biographies of men like Jim Thorpe or Jesse Owens.

Very good rapport was established, and the students identified positively with the coach, who stimulated their areas of strength and interest. From this stimulation there gradually flowed more interest in the learning and academic areas, and the coach led the boys into reinvolvement with school learning. Of this group, only one boy dropped out, but his problems were compounded by a worsening home situation.

In both case studies cited, the consultant functioned as a resource person for the teacher. The small group approach was demonstrated first by the consultant who worked directly with the group of students. The teacher was an observer at first and then a co-leader. The consultant then pulled out, and the teacher conducted the group sessions. Other teachers expressed interest and wanted to take on group sessions as long as they knew that they had the backing of the consultant.

CARETAKERS

Indirect Consultation

In the indirect approach the consultant does not see the student or students. Instead he works directly with school personnel (or others) who in turn work with the students. In general this approach is more widely used and by far the more popular approach in school mental health consultation. Many consultants favor this approach based on past experience. The indirect approach makes the optimal use of the consultant's time.

In the direct consultation a consultant can spend the afternoon evaluating four youngsters in four hours and share these observations with the youngsters' teachers. His time may be better used if he spent those four hours in indirect consultation, meeting with groups of teachers or other school personnel. The teachers could then apply the consultant's understanding to the entire classroom and not to just one child. Instead of helping just four children, many others could be helped by this approach.

If the objective of mental health consultation in the schools is to help the learning child, the indirect approach is the most satisfactory in reaching a greater number of children. The consultant can help teachers develop strengths in understanding the emotional aspects of learning, enhance their knowledge of child development, help them develop understanding of influences that affect the learning child, and help modify attitudes to reflect good learning and good mental health.

Consultation with Parents

One of the major areas in which indirect consultation is applicable is with parents. Whatever impact is made on parents can be transferred to students. Consultants can work with groups of parents in many problem areas. For example, a group of parents of children with perceptual motor problems met weekly with a consultant. The objective of the program was to involve the parents in helping their children. Previously the students were seen as failures, and the parents were becoming very detached from the school because of a sense of frustration and failure.

In another school, this time a ghetto elementary school, the consultant found that many of the worst discipline problems came from homes in which parents had such negative attitudes toward school that they were actually anti-school. All their contacts with the school had centered on their children as troublemakers. It was felt that there would be very little effective change in the children without a change in parental attitudes. A parents' group was organized, not on a negative basis to call attention to their role as parents of troublemakers, but to help parents understand children of this age. The school principal invited the parents to take part in a program entitled "What Ten-year-old Children are Like at Home and School." The parents were having as much trouble as the school with their children, and the appeal of the program was to try to help the parents with many of the problems they were having with the children at home.

In presenting the program in a positive way, the group of parents responded in a similar manner and the program helped to bring an alliance between the classroom teacher and the parents, rather than two distinct enemy camps. The program was meant to give parents support, and the parents responded to the support by changing some of their attitudes toward their children and the school. This was facilitated by a series of meetings for the parents led by a classroom teacher and a mental health consultant.

Consultations with Community Organizations

Another area for consultation can be an ancillary community organization which exerts an influence on the learning child. The YMCA, YWCA, a settlement house, Boys' Club, or other youth organizations all have an impact on students, and people from these agencies can be effective in helping children. In most cases the consultant will deal with these community agents in conjunction with the school personnel. For example, there was an area where a considerable number of boys who were having difficulties in school came from fatherless homes. One effective part of consultation with school personnel was to involve representatives from local community agencies such as Big Brother and the YMCA. The elementary school had an almost all female faculty, and the use of male adults from these agencies enabled some help for these students which consultation was able to coordinate and support.

Consultation with School Personnel

Consultation with the school personnel as the child caretaker is by far the most popular form of school mental health consultation. This indirect form of consultation, as already stated, makes the optimal use of consultation time and impact. In general the consultation with school personnel can be essentially topic or subject oriented, case conference oriented, or informal and open-ended.

In the situation where the model of consultation centers

around specific topics of interest, one might consider such topics as learning disabilities, management of disciplinary problems, stealing, and drug abuse. Here the consultant would focus on a subject rather than on specific students. A frequently sought after topic has been the various aspects of child development and each meeting might be devoted to dealing with problems related to different stages of child development. This may help teachers learn more about children and apply this knowledge to the classroom situation. Although subject and topic consultation may be requested by teachers, I have found that it is often not very rewarding. It may be interesting and intellectually stimulating but, on a pragmatic level, often produces very little change in the classroom climate or in helping children with particular problems. One example that was an exception to this was an experience where this model went beyond just discussing various subjects. The teachers got actively involved and researched all they could about students whom they felt were stereotypes and examples of the subject discussed, e.g. students who came to their mind because of immaturity and underachieving. In so doing, the teachers not only learned more about the subject, but got to know much more about the student and then were able to practically apply what was brought in and discussed in the consultation session.

In the model of open-ended consultation, the main goal here is to provide the school personnel with a consultant who can be available to deal with whatever is bugging them. This vehicle allows the teachers or other school personnel to discuss with the consultant the things that are making them most anxious and giving them the most difficulty. This can be a very helpful type of consultation, although many times because of the spontaneity involved, the consultant may be of limited help. One example of this type of consultation was a situation where the consultant arranged with a particular elementary school that he would spend one afternoon every two weeks in that school to meet with anyone who wished to talk with him about anything that was on their minds. This helped considerably to ease a lot of the tension that was in the school, improve staff morale, and establish a more trusting relationship between the teachers and the consultant. From this type of consultation, the case conference model later evolved.

The case conference consultation model is probably the most popular type of consultation with school personnel. This type of consultation centers around specific youngsters, helping school personnel to better understand how they can adapt to the youngster, and how the youngster can adapt to school. Since this model is so widely used and one which I definitely prefer, it will be discussed in detail in the next chapter.

CONSULTATION TO THE SCHOOL PROGRAM

In addition to focusing consultation directly with the student or indirectly with the child caretakers, consultation may focus primarily on the school program. In this area, attention can be centered on various policies and programs in the school and how they may affect the students. For example, the consultant might work with the school administrators who are involved in establishing the curriculum or school policies. Discussion will touch on areas that affect learning and attitudes. One example of this type of consultation is where the school board decided to introduce sex education into their curriculum. The consultant, as a specialist in child development, was extremely helpful to the school in establishing a curriculum that not only focused on the cognitive aspects, but also on the affective factors.

CONSULTATION BASED ON LEVELS OF PREVENTION

In addition to consultation being based on specific components of the school system, as described above, consultation models may also be based on various levels of prevention. Gerald Caplan in his book, *The Principles of Preventive Psychiatry*, very aptly describes primary, secondary, and tertiary levels of prevention. The primary level of prevention is the discovery, control and elimination of *potential* areas of breakdown. Secondary prevention is described as the early detection, diagnosis, and prompt treatment of conditions that have already begun to manifest disturbance. Tertiary prevention is described as attempts to reduce impairment that has already been suffered in disturbances and conditions that have continued and not received earlier intervention. This focus is more at the level of rehabilitation.

An example of these various levels of prevention in medicine could be, for instance, the situation with tuberculosis. Primary prevention would be the screening and vaccination of children as part of routine medical care to discover any early signs of tuberculosis or in situations where the potential for it to occur is more likely, e.g. another member of the family has known tuberculosis. If no primary prevention was done and now a youngster manifests early signs of the illness such as a cough, nightly fevers and sweats, then early diagnosis of his having tuberculosis and prompt therapy would be part of secondary prevention. If no primary and secondary prevention has taken place, and the youngster has not been helped, then we now might find a situation where a child has far more advanced tuberculosis and is having more chronic symptoms of impairment and might need long-term hospitalization, surgery, and rehabilitation.

In education, we may look at the development of reading disability as an example of where primary, secondary, and tertiary prevention principles could be applied. In primary prevention, screening programs and programs to develop a child's enrichment and potential to learn on a preschool level could be viewed as primary prevention. We are still dealing with a population that has not demonstrated any reading disability but are concerned in the potential of this coming event. An example of the secondary prevention level would be where the same child is now in first or second grade and is showing signs of reading difficulty. Here, identifying the reading difficulty, evaluating its cause (for instance, perceptual motor problems), and instituting immediate and prompt help (for instance, motor training or coordination training), will help deal with the situation. If on the other hand, there has been no dealing with potential reading disability, and there has been no intervention in terms of early diagnosis and remediation on the secondary level, then we may end up with a youngster who is now in the fifth grade with a marked and long-standing reading disability (perhaps reading on a second grade level) and also now manifesting secondary emotional and behavioral problems because of his reading disability. At this point, we are beyond simple immediate remediation and might have to be involved in much more difficult and expensive rehabilitative measures such as a specialized class placement in a learning disabilities class, considerable tutoring, and help with the secondary emotional problems.

In most cases, the school seeks consultation first on the tertiary level because of the long-standing problems. These problems generally are children known to the entire school. They are the villains, the nemeses of the school and the headache of the principal. The school may want immediate help with these children. At this point, the consultant may see what help he can provide in this situation. However, at the same time he may try to use these long-standing problems as examples to stress the necessity for intervention on secondary or primary levels in order to prevent this type of severe problem continually recurring.

For example, in one situation, a sixth grade youngster was manifesting severe behavior problems. He was disruptive, defiant, belligerent, and destructive. In discussion the consultant learned that the kindergarten teacher had noted that he exhibited immaturities and difficulties in working in group situations, had poor attention span, and extreme tension. These were all factors affecting his inability to successfully cope with learning. His subsequent teachers all noted similar problems. Yet, basically, all that was done was to note and to record. Nothing was done in the way of any effective intervention. So now help is sought at the sixth grade level where the problem is chronic, long-standing, and on the tertiary level. In this case, the consultant helped the teachers to realize and identify with the very strong feelings of inadequacy the student had and his frustration in trying to cope with unrealistic expectations. Once this was established, intensive remedial reading help was instituted, a school counselor was assigned to help be an aide to the student with whatever problems came up in school, and outside therapy was recommended to help deal with many of the emotional problems that had evolved. Thus the consultant was of limited help in this particular situation, but it was a springboard as an example of how situations like this could be prevented if consultation had been instituted back in the first grade at a secondary prevention level.

Many times a consultant will have to start consultation around the most severe problems in the school, but hopefully, this approach will only be used as a means of getting to more workable and less severe problems, and concentration will be on the value of preventive programs. When the contract drawn up by the school seeks to put emphasis on direct consultation service contrary to the consultant's wish to build a preventive program, the objective of the consultant is to find a workable balance between the two extremes in order to avoid an overemphasis of one at the expense of the other. If the consultant overemphasizes the in-service training aspect and neglects some of the service needs, the school will become disenchanted with him, feeling that he is not really a helpful ally. He might not remain in that system too much longer.

On the other hand, if the school is interested only in dealing with crises or "putting out fires" and does not share the consultant's concern about in-service training, there will be very little growth on the part of the school staff and the consultant will feel he is being used by the school and not part of a mutual collaboration towards helping the school child.

Hopefully, the ideal goal of consultation is that it be so effective and on such preventive levels that it will eventually do away with the need for the consultation itself, and that the school personnel could then handle the problems themselves.

One of the main reasons for the popularity of the case conference consultation is that it comes closest to resolving the aforementioned conflict. If handled properly, the case conference can be the vehicle serving both needs because the consultation centers on actual youngsters about whom teachers are concerned thus meeting some of the service needs of the school. At the same time, the consultation can be used as a springboard for in-service training in the areas of learning, child development, and preventive measures. The case conference can provide a method of meeting both goals and integrating them through one approach.

Many times the success of a consultation program can be

measured by the diminishing discussion of children on the tertiary level. The school copes with them as best they can and begins to use the consultant for help on the secondary and primary levels of prevention. For example, the principal will say, "Let's not talk about Frankie because we really will be wasting the consultant's time. We know he's a severe problem and we are doing what we can to help him. Let's talk about Willie who's just beginning to show signs of problems and see what we can do to prevent him from becoming a severe problem and another Frankie."

To measure success in another way, it is important to remember that the method or approach used should help the teacher feel more comfortable in her role. If the teacher feels positive about her role, almost inevitably the child will be helped. This general rule of thumb also applies to the consultant. If the consultant feels good about the consultation, then he can usually assume that the consultee felt the same way, and some help was delivered.

CHAPTER **6**

THE CASE
CONSULTATION MODEL

A<small>S HAS ALREADY BEEN MENTIONED</small>, the case consultation approach is a very popular one, widely used by mental health consultants in the schools. One of the main reasons for its popularity is that it is an excellent vehicle for trying to resolve the conflict of meeting service needs of the school on one hand and trying to build in preventive measures on the other hand. Through various consultation approaches and by trial and error, I have come to heavily favor and extensively use this approach.

The mainstay of the case consultation approach is the case conference. The goal of this conference is to arrive at an *interactional diagnosis*. When working toward meeting this goal, the consultant serves two purposes. The first is as a catalyst to group participation and interaction, and the second is as a resource person in areas where his expertise is needed.

By interactional diagnosis, we mean that rather than simply diagnose a child as neurotic, psychotic or hyperkinetic and rather than arrive at what might be wrong in what the teacher is doing, the objective is to arrive at a diagnosis of the problems in the student-teacher interaction itself. If the diagnosis centers on the manifestations of the child's problems in his relationship with the teacher, and the teacher sees those manifestations and the reason for them, she then can learn to deal with them better. For that reason the consultation session should dwell not only on what is going on with the child but also how the teacher is reacting and dealing with the problem.

For example, if the interactional diagnosis is one of anxiety on the student's part in relation to any authority figure, the teacher can realize that whatever the symptoms of the anxiety are, the anxiety is due basically to the student's fear of her in her role as an authority. The teacher then can use her own approaches and resources to find ways to alleviate the student's anxiety along with the suggestions that the consultant and her fellow teachers may provide.

Another value of this approach is that it provides the teacher with an avenue for concrete alternatives to try to help the interaction between her and the student rather than provide a purely academic or theoretical understanding of the youngster. This type of diagnosis also provides for ways of mutual adaptation—the child might be helped to adapt to the school, and the school and the teacher might be helped to adapt to the problem youngster.

Through seeking such an interactional diagnosis, a model has evolved that not only applies to the student discussed but also has application to other similar students. Thus it has some universal value.

Essentially, the consultation session is directed to three main areas: The first is sharing information and observations about the student, both in the classroom and with the teachers; the second is the establishment of the interactional diagnosis, and the third is the resulting psycho-educational recommendations. That is, recommendations involving psychological, emotional, and social factors that will be translated into meaningful recommendations that can be carried out in the educational setting.

For example, the psychological diagnosis is that a youngster who has very strong competitive feelings and because of various factors, feels that he's second rate, cannot successfully compete. In the educational translation and application, the recommendation is to foster situations that are noncompetitive so that the child's feeling of inability to compete (so why bother), is removed. The teacher might set up situations that are competitive but designed so the child can compete successfully. For instance, a student may be very inadequate in physical education but very adequate in art. The teacher would then find some way to help the student "show his stuff" in art.

At this point it may be helpful to outline a prototype of an ideal consultation session. By no means, however, is this prototype the one and only model; nevertheless, it is an effective one.

THE STRUCTURE

In general the consultation session should be about two hours in length, and as pointed out earlier, the consultant can be from any of the mental health disciplines: psychology, social work, or psychiatry. The consultee group is composed of school personnel and the group can be from any category: teachers, principals, pupil personnel workers.

A good workable group size is about eight to ten persons including both the consultant and the consultees. If the group is very much larger, it often does not permit sufficient group participation and can even inhibit members from speaking. On the other hand, if a group is much smaller, it does not allow enough cross-section of viewpoints needed to foster good group interaction and recommendations.

One mechanical aspect of case consultation that has proved extremely useful is the formality of keeping minutes. The minutes will provide a written record of the discussion which can be used for research on trends, processes, or changes over a period of time. Minutes also can be distributed to absent principals or other administrators who will be involved in the recommendations resulting from the sessions. It's a handy way to reach a wider audience.

Minutes will not break confidentiality if specific children are not mentioned by name. The minutes simply discuss the nature of the problem, diagnosis, and conclusions. Information of a very personal nature does not have to be included.

It is suggested that participants take turns keeping the minutes. It is an extremely valuable tool in helping them conceptualize and digest information gleaned in the consultation session. Interestingly enough, consultees at first take verbatim reports. Later the minutes reflect that the consultees have learned to synthesize and integrate the information.

THE PROCESS

An actual case consultation session can be divided into four phases. The first phase is the actual presentation of case material by the teacher. In the second phase the consultant acts as a resource person, translating this material into an emotional understanding of the child in the learning situation and arriving at an interactional diagnosis. In the third phase, the consultant and consultees will work together to arrive at recommendations. The fourth and final phase is the wrap-up by the consultant.

Let's look at each of the four phases in detail. The initial part of the two-hour consultation session centers on the presentation of the case. At this time the consultee presents information on a student about whom she is concerned. The case presentation serves a dual purpose: First, it provides consultation on the problems and concerns that teachers might have, and second, it provides a springboard for in-service training and learning that may be applicable to other children and to the whole sphere of learning and child development.

It is important for the consultee to avoid presenting the initial information on the child as a monologue as the objective is to effect group process. It must allow other consultees in the group to make comments, ask questions, give feedback and reactions. Often, however, the group interaction has to be initiated and stimulated by the consultant. The initial presentation will provide a skeleton of the nature of the problem, and the participants are invited to add muscle and substance to the skeleton by asking questions and offering impressions drawn from their own experience.

The first phase of the consultation has been completed when a picture of the child has been presented, teacher responses have been obtained, and a cohesive picture of the interaction between the child and teacher has been drawn.

During this phase which usually takes about one hour, the consultant plays the role of a catalyst in order to see that an outline is presented to the group to which they can add, and to promote group process and interaction.

In the second phase of the session, usually lasting thirty minutes, the consultant plays the role of a resource person. He helps to translate the picture of the child into the area of his own expertise. That is, the area of child development, child psychology, and any other social or biological aspect. The resource person weaves all of the information into an understanding of the total child and makes an interactional diagnosis. At this point the consultees are encouraged to react to the diagnosis according to their own impressions. This sets the stage for the third phase of the session, namely, the discussing of educational recommendations (which adds about thirty minutes to the session).

Using the picture of the total child, the consultees can now better translate this information into educational recommendations. Let's take an example in which the picture of the child includes feelings of marked inferiority and strong dependency on the emotional level, short stature and poor coordination on the biological level, and a home situation in which inadequacies have been strongly reinforced on the social level. Based on this information, the consultee can come up with educational recommendations that will try to decrease the feelings of inadequacy, will minimize and underplay biological deficits, and will try to diminish whatever social reinforcement there has been of these inadequacies. The entire group will participate in making the recommendations.

The fourth and final phase is the wrap-up, lasting about fifteen minutes in length, in which the consultant summarizes the main points of the total picture and emphasizes the recommendations that have evolved. This helps the consultees reintegrate what has taken place during the session.

REACTIONS TO CASE CONSULTATION

Surprisingly enough, often after a consultation session a teacher has said, "I thought I was the only one who had that problem." She's surprised to hear that other teachers share the same kinds of problems. Consultation helps to alleviate this feeling of being alone, and it gives teachers more self-awareness and has often relieved feelings of inadequacy about themselves. This is all related to giving them more self-acceptance; anything that helps the teacher feel more comfortable and more self-confident is going to pay off for the student.

There are various kinds of responses that indicate the effectiveness of a consultation session. When a consultee leaves a meeting saying, "That was a very interesting session," often this is an indication that the consultant has been too didactic or too psychoanalytical. As a result, there has been only limited group interaction with little in the way of practical help.

Conversely, if the consultee says, "That was of no help to us," the consultant was not active enough or was not a helpful catalyst and resource person. The group will feel that they had to do it all on their own and found out what they already knew.

4. What kinds of feelings do these symptoms invoke in you?
5. When do these symptoms usually occur (e.g. time of day?)
6. Where do they usually occur?
7. With whom do they usually occur? (teacher, peers, etc.)
8. What seems to aggravate these symptoms?
9. What seems to alleviate these symptoms?
10. How does the student seem to feel as to why this is happening?
11. How do you, the teacher, seem to feel as to why this is happening?

III. EDUCABILITY OF STUDENT (His capacity to learn)

A. Intelligence?
B. Physical capacities
   1. General health and nutrition?
   2. Sensory abilities (Auditory, Visual)?
   3. Neurological disturbances (motor defects, brain damage, etc.)
C. Maturity (independence, interests, self-control, etc.)
D. Motivation
   1. Attitudes and feelings toward learning?
   2. Feelings about himself (self-concept).
   3. Attitude toward teacher?
   4. Attitude toward classmates and peers?
   5. Attitude about parents' value on education?
   6. Attitude about siblings' performance as students?
E. Inner freedom to learn? (Child's fears, anxieties, fantasies, daydreams, etc.)
F. Opportunity to learn? (Class climate, class size, external distractions, setting to do homework, etc.)
G. Past school history? (Previous teacher's comments, performance in earlier grades, achievement level at time of entering your class)

IV. DEVELOPMENTAL HISTORY (How did problems start? Was it always this way? etc.)

    A. Pregnancy? (planned, unplanned, adopted, etc.)

    B. Any significant birth history? (e.g. any congenital defects, etc.)

    C. Mastery of various developmental skills? (sitting, walking, talking, toilet training, etc.)

    D. How did child cope with normal developmental crises? (birth of siblings, family moves, separations from mother, illness, onset of puberty, etc.)

    E. How did child cope with abnormal developmental crises (death of parents or sibling, divorce or desertion of parents, crippling or disfiguring illness, major family problems, e.g. drinking?)

V. BACKGROUND INFORMATION

    A. Family Background

        1. General home atmosphere?

        2. Parents' background (education, occupation, values, interests, etc.) ?

        3. Status of siblings (successes and failures?)

        4. Relationship and interaction between mother and child?

        5. Relationship and interaction between father and child?

        6. Relationship and interaction between siblings and child?

    B. Social relationships? (neighborhood, peers, authority figures, etc.)

    C. Any other significant environmental factors not included above?

VI. A. In extracting information from this model (items I to V), what do you consider the significant items? Please list.

B. Taking these items together, what do you therefore consider the major problem or problems in the learning-teaching interaction?

Various parts of this worksheet warrant further elaboration and clarification. The first three categories of this model have a common denominator; namely, all the information presented here can be obtained solely from the teacher's classroom observations and records and are not contingent on any outside sources. Nevertheless, in most cases meaningful consultation and recommendations can result.

THE FIRST ITEM IS THE IDENTIFYING DATA. The picture should be hopefully complete enough to allow other participants to pinpoint the child if they walked into the teacher's classroom. This of course is the ideal goal.

The value of this identifying data is that it gives a base orientation upon which subsequent information can be superimposed, and it also leads to various speculations about the youngster. For example, if we hear that this student is the youngest of four children, we will probably start to wonder whether this child has been treated as the baby of the family and might be overly immature and dependent.

On the other hand, if we hear that the student is hyperactive, restless, and "all over the place," then we might speculate that we are going to hear about a child who might be hyperkinetic or perhaps be in the general category of minimal brain dysfunction.

THE SECOND CATEGORY IS THE TEACHER'S CONCERN AND IMPRESSIONS ABOUT THE PROBLEM. Here the teacher tells why she is concerned and why she is seeking help from her fellow consultees and the consultant. In describing the symptoms, it is helpful to have the teacher also present information on what precedes the onset of the symptoms, what goes on during their manifestations, and what happens afterward.

For example, if we learn that the teacher's concern is devices such as calling out or clowning, we might learn that preceding these actions, the teacher has become very involved with another student and has ignored this student and the rest of the class. We might find that the teacher responds to this kind of behavior even if it is in the form of some kind of an admonishment. This before, during and after description helps us to recognize the child's need to seek attention.

Another aspect of the teacher's concern, aside from focusing on the symptom itself, is her own actions before, during, and after the student's actions. We can see its relevance in the previous example. This information might shed more light on the ways in which the handling of a situation might help to reinforce or extinguish this symptomatic behavior.

It is very helpful to know how the teacher feels about her reaction to the symptom. For instance, we may hear of a youngster who gets very aggressive, overactive, and destructive. However, the teacher says that she often feels sorry for him. Then we might wonder if this is an expression of anxiety in the student over which he has no control and the teacher recognizes this and responds with empathy or sympathy. On the other hand, another youngster with basically the same kinds of symptoms makes the teacher very angry. This might be a diagnostic clue that this is behavior that the student has voluntary control over, and the teacher feels that he could "help himself and not have to do it." Thus, the teacher might not be able to diagnose the meaning of the symptom, but her own feelings and responses can be a very helpful diagnostic clue.

When you want the teacher to identify with the feelings of the youngster, the consultation is much more successful if it stimulates the feelings of the teacher and is not merely an intellectual experience for the teacher. In other words, in order to mobilize feelings on the teacher's part towards the student, the consultant has to mobilize feelings in the teacher about herself and maybe about the consultant. If the consultation is purely intellectual, then the teacher views the child the same way and there will be no attitude change. It is quite obvious to the consultant whether the teacher is talking about a youngster or feeling for him.

One good way to stimulate feelings in the teacher is to try to find a personal experience or any other experience that can be translated into what the child is experiencing. Try to help the teacher identify with the child's situation by bringing out something the teacher has gone through. The consultant can then turn to the teacher and say, "You see how you feel there. Well, that's just the way this kid feels." If you bring the child's frame of reference into the teacher's perspective, the teacher can identify with him.

One technique is to say to teachers, "Just think for a minute about the teacher you liked the best when you were a student." Very often they will say their choice is the teacher who in some way conveyed to them that they liked them and respected them. When this comes out, the consultant says, "And what do you think will help this student who doesn't have enough self-esteem and self-respect?"

In expressing her concern for the student, the teacher also should elaborate on the factors associated with the symptomatic behavior such as what kinds of things aggravate it, what diminishes it, when and where the symptoms occur, and in whose presence. If we learn that the student's behavioral outburst occurs only toward the end of the day, we might wonder whether this condition is related to fatigue in some way and a low tolerance for frustration at that point. And if behavior symptoms occur only when the student is in a coeducational situation, it might have something to do with sexual anxieties and/or feelings of inadequacy in the presence of the opposite sex.

In the Third Category, We Need a Basic Picture of the Student's Capacity to Learn—His Educability. What we try to do here is to see how qualified he is to be in that particular classroom and learning situation. In assessing his educability, we need to look at the biological, psychological, and social spheres. It gives us a total picture of the child and not simply his IQ or his attitude.

The following subdivisions are areas for the teacher to observe and report to the group.

Impressions of Intellectual Capacity

In this case you might say that the IQ is needed in order to supply this information and, indeed, this can be helpful. However, any experienced teacher can get a fairly accurate idea of a student's intellectual capacity just from her own observations. This has been acknowledged by many teachers.

Physical and Biological Capacities

Here the teacher should report on any seeming deficits in this area, e.g. is the child hampered by poor vision, a neurologic problem, possible epilepsy, or a visual motor problem?

Maturity

Again from her own observations, the teacher can get a fairly accurate assessment of the student's emotional maturity, especially his degree of independence, his autonomy, and his level of interest toward academic tasks and learning. For instance, if the teacher reports that the youngster is interested only in play activities and has very little interest in work, this is a statement of some immaturity.

Motivation

From her own observations the teacher can get a fairly good picture of how motivated a student is toward learning. Not sufficiently recognized is the importance of obtaining information about the student's feelings toward himself (his self-concept), toward his teacher, his classmates, and his parents or siblings which might be transferred into the learning situation positively or negatively. In addition, any information about the student's feeling toward learning, the curriculum, and the school can shed more light on his motivation. This is especially true where we find some very bright students who have very poor motivation toward learning because they feel that the curriculum is irrelevant or they feel that the school is too establishment-oriented or too impersonal. If the youngster comes from a home where learning is not highly prized or highly valued, then this attitude might be transferred to the school situation.

A boy's motivation toward trying to achieve in school can be affected significantly if his peer group considers learning and academic achievement to be sissy, and the regular guys don't do well in school. Needless to say, probably the most significant factor in learning is the feelings a student has about himself, and here we are particularly concerned about his self-esteem, his self-confidence, and his self-reliance.

Freedom to Learn

What are the internal factors in the learning situation? Often this area is not sufficiently appreciated although it can be observed by the teacher. Does the student have sufficient peace of mind and concentration to focus on learning? That is, does he have fears, anxieties, or fantasies that inhibit this freedom to learn? From the standpoint of his internal psychological makeup, is he free to be open and receptive to what is presented to him? Often it is helpful to have the teacher bring in samples of the student's essays, writings, or drawings. Sometimes this is an excellent way to get a picture of the student's internal self. Needless to say, any available psychological testing would be very helpful here.

Opportunity to Learn

What are the external factors in the learning situation? In this area we try to get some idea of the climate of the classroom—the noise level, the size. At times this might be significant for a particular youngster. If a shy, rather passive and easily intimidated student is in the same class with very boisterous and tough boys, he might feel so intimidated by their close physical presence that he might not have much of an opportunity to learn.

All these items can be furnished on the basis of the teacher's classroom observations. Very often at this point in the presentation, if this information has been supplied, we have a working hypothesis about the problem. In addition, information about the teacher-student interaction is opening the door to later teacher applicable recommendations.

The subsequent information goes beyond the teacher's classroom observations and is dependent upon other sources. This information often is not available at all or in far less depth and detail than listed below. Both the consultant and consultee have to realize this and make do with whatever information they have. This kind of information can be obtained in part from the student's permanent record, health record, home visits, parent conferences, psychological tests, social worker reports, and reports of other facilities.

DEVELOPMENTAL HISTORY.   From the information given to this point we should have a good idea of the problem of the student in the classroom. It would be very helpful now to get some idea of how and when the problem started. Obviously, if the student is off the track at this point, it would be helpful to find out how and when he derailed inasmuch as this might have an impact on the corrective and remedial measures.

We are particularly interested in developmental history, not only in abnormal crises such as a broken home, death of a parent, or a severe accident or illness, but also in the normal crises of child development such as separation at the start of kindergarten or first grade, reaction to the birth of siblings, or onset of adolescence.

It is important to stress this area because the teacher might be very quick to overemphasize any unusual or abnormal situation in the child's development. At the same time, knowing how the child handled other milestones of normal growth and development can also be very significant. For example, in arriving at a diagnosis of school phobia, knowledge of how earlier child-parent separations were handled is most relevant.

Next we are interested in the preschool period from two to four years of age, when the youngster began to lean more toward others and became a more social person. We are primarily concerned with how he seemed to develop peer relationships and interaction with other people, and his degree of independence.

Information on the school period should include nursery school, kindergarten, and subsequent grades. The school picture, although primarily focused on academic performance, also should include behavioral and social aspects. It is helpful to have records available to trace any organic problems such as congenital abnormalities, neurological problems, serious illnesses, and surgery.

Basically an attempt is being made to get a picture of how the child developed biologically, psychologically, and socially.

PICTURE OF BACKGROUND AND ENVIRONMENT OF THE STUDENT. Information also should be obtained about the student's family situation, neighbor and community relationships, and social relationships. Their relevance is so obvious that no further elaboration is necessary.

Once the five items previously listed have been presented, the consultation group now can arrive at an interactional diagnosis in most cases. There will be an understanding of the problem between the student and teacher which causes the teacher to have this degree of concern and, hopefully, how it came about.

Thus having arrived at the interactional diagnosis, now in Phase II, the consultant can serve as a resource person and tie everything together. One model which I have found very helpful is to view the material presented in the form of a three-layered cake. The top layer is the symptoms and concerns which the teacher has expressed. The middle layer is the student's feelings which appear to produce the symptoms. The bottom layer is the factors and events in the student's life, both past and present, that have produced these feelings. For example, if the symptoms of the child presented were "very defensive, can't take criticism, gives up as soon as the work gets hard, will never ask for help, and pouts and withdraws if he can't succeed," then I would go to the next level and point out the obvious feelings of inadequacy that the student has in the academic sphere and his fears of being exposed and seen as stupid. We may then find that on the bottom level, this student was one who has older siblings who have always been outstanding academically, but he himself got off to a poor start because of a minor perceptual problem and difficulty in reading, and that as the youngest in his family, he is often referred to as "a kid who doesn't know anything, so just keep quiet." This brief example integrating the symptoms, feelings, and their causes is a model which permits the teachers to not only understand, but often to identify with what the student is going through. This will then allow for more meaningful suggestions in the third phase where the teachers and participants attempt to make psycho-educational recommendations. The consultees will not just be looking for management of symptoms or symptom removal, but also attempting to help with the child's feelings and the factors that produced them. They will thus be trying to help the total child and not just classroom performance.

Hopefully, in Phase III, there will be free and open discussion with participants expressing their own thoughts and suggestions as to how to help the teacher and student. It is important during this that the consultee is encouraging and supportive. It is the consultant's function to help create the kind of climate that will permit free interchange and not one where a teacher will be afraid to express herself, because she doesn't want anyone to think she doesn't know enough.

In Phase IV of the consultation session, namely the wrap-up, the consultant tries to sum up and help reintegrate what has been discussed. This is often quite necessary because of the large amount of material that might have been presented and because of many digressions that might have taken place as part of the open discussion.

THE LANGUAGE IN THE CASE CONFERENCE

In the identifying data, the consultant might ask the group, "What do you think is going on with this child?" when the consultee notes that the student never looks a person in the eye, often has his head down, or walks with his shoulders slumped. Not only is this approach designed to get group interaction and group response, but also to elicit whatever speculation the consultees have about the student at that moment. This then stimulates their interest because now they're going to listen to see if this impression is substantiated by further information. In a sense, it's got them a "little hooked."

The consultees are going to be more interested because they will want to test out their early hypotheses. This can be done repeatedly in many different ways. If the teacher responds in a certain way after the symptom is expressed and the group is asked at that point what they're thinking, the consultant might find that various teachers in the group are beginning to have contrasting thoughts in response to what is going on. This then can be the beginning of the groundwork for later recommendations.

For example, the teacher knows that John, a student with little self-confidence, brings up irrelevant questions and comments when he is being given help on a one-to-one basis when the work begins to get hard. In the middle of an explanation, he'll say, "Do you know what I got for my birthday?" or "Do you know what I'm going to get for Christmas?" When this happens the teacher's response usually was, "Well, look, let's keep our mind on our work," or "Let's talk about that later," or something to that effect. However, she has found that this response didn't seem to help much.

When the group was asked for their impressions at this point, another teacher said, "I wonder if he's doing this when he is trying to work hard and is getting anxious, and if the teacher were to let him know that she recognizes this, it might relieve some of the anxiety." Instead of saying, "Let's go on with our work," or "Let's talk about it later," she might say, "Gee, you're asking about what you're going to get for Christmas. I know what we're doing is pretty hard, and I wonder whether you're feeling that way, too!" This is letting the student know that the teacher recognizes his problem. The student then might express his concern that it is hard, and the teacher can now let him know that she recognizes it, accepts it, and will now help him with it. This will not only relieve anxiety but also promote a more positive learning situation.

When the second teacher made her suggestion, the teacher who was presenting the case said, "Oh, that's a good idea. I never thought of doing that because I thought the less fuss, the less attention I paid to this kid's manipulation (she recognized it as a device) was the best way to handle it." She had never really thought of stopping and really paying attention to the child's feelings of anxiety underlying the manipulative attempt to mask it.

A major mistake on the consultant's part would be to try to impose his way of doing something on the consultee. Instead, he should try to introduce a new concept or a different way of looking at something, and then leave it up to the consultee to apply it in a way that is most comfortable. In a case in which the consultant introduces the concept of more initiative and responsibility for a student who is immature and too dependent, he should let the teacher find a method that she can apply comfortably; it might be by letting the child be a monitor or allowing the child to help with certain tasks. If the consultant specifically prescribes the ways for the teacher to apply the concept and this is not comfortable for the teacher, then the consultant is not being very helpful to the teacher and the teacher might feel she is a failure.

CHAPTER 7

THE TEACHER BACK IN
THE CLASSROOM

No MATTER how enlightening or helpful the consultation session may be, the teacher must be able to translate what she learns in the consultation process into her relationship with her students back in the classroom.

To be successful, the consultation session must enable the teacher to become a collaborator with the students so that they can work together in the areas on which the consultation focused. In order for this to take place, there must be a collaborative feeling, a feeling of mutual respect, both for the teacher as an educator and the student as a learner, and there must be a willingness to adapt to each other.

Of course, no one will argue with this idea; nonetheless, there are many conflicts and other personal and interpersonal problems that interfere with the establishment of a climate that permits the application of consultation recommendations. It is very helpful for the teacher to have an awareness of some of these overt and covert obstacles hindering this kind of working relationship, and it is very helpful for the consultant to be aware of them too. If these obstacles are not recognized by both the consultant and consultee, there might be unnecessary premature feelings of frustration and failure because the consultation recommendations are not immediately successful.

An appreciation of these obstacles will temper any disappointment and will point up the need for follow-up to help the teacher with some of the problems that might be present in the relationship with the student. In Chapter 3, I discussed obstacles in the consultation process itself, whereas these are obstacles in carrying out the consultation recommendations.

What are these obstacles?

THE TEACHER WHO HAS NOT CLEARLY WORKED OUT THE

DIFFERENCE BETWEEN BEING AN AUTHORITY AND BEING AUTHORITARIAN. The teacher who sees herself as an authority acknowledges that she has some expertise in the area she is teaching, but this does not mean that she can now be authoritarian. The teacher who sees herself as an authority promotes positive identification by the student with her expertise and possibly stimulates the student to want some of this knowledge for himself. On the other hand, the teacher who comes across as authoritarian, because she thinks she is an authority, can instill anti-learning attitudes in the student such as fear, rebellion, and submission. This authoritarian attitude may be expressed as "I know more than you; therefore, shut-up and listen."

VALUE SYSTEM DIFFERENCES BETWEEN THE TEACHER AND STUDENT MIGHT INTERFERE WITH ATTAINING AN ATMOSPHERE OF MUTUAL RESPECT. Ideally, the teacher will try not to impose her value system on the student nor the student on the teacher. Sometimes teachers are so obsessed with certain values such as cleanliness, meticulousness and tidiness that it interferes with their application of the consultation recommendations.

In a particular case one of the recommendations made to the teacher was to try in any way to praise and reward the student's endeavors. Due to disorganization and anxiety, the student had difficulty in presenting his ideas. The teacher followed the recommendation by praising the student's ideas in composition. However, the student continued to see himself as a failure because his papers came back studded with spelling and grammar corrections because of the teacher's inability to tolerate grammatical errors.

CONFLICT WITHIN THE TEACHER IN THE AREA OF DEPENDENCY-INDEPENDENCY. For instance, if part of the consultation recommendation has been to promote more autonomy and independent functioning in the student, the teacher might go along with this intellectually. However, if she has a great need to have the student dependent upon her, thus making her a very needed and important person, she might unknowingly promote this dependency at a covert level while overtly believing that she is promoting independence.

The converse can be true, too. The recommendations might be that a child needs to be more dependent and the teacher appreciates this fact, but she cannot tolerate dependency and sees it as an infantile state. This teacher might have great difficulty in allowing a student to be dependent on her even though it is recommended.

THEN THERE'S THE TEACHER WHO HAS A CONFLICT BETWEEN A CHILD-ORIENTED APPROACH VS. A CURRICULUM-ORIENTED APPROACH. If the teacher has a compulsive and obsessive need to follow the lesson plan, she will be hindered in performing in a flexible way that might bolster the student's self-esteem and other needs that were pointed out in the consultation. Let's call this teacher "one who feels *what* is being learned takes precedence over *who* is being taught." This is the teacher who has a conflict between her need to teach concepts and at the same time acknowledge a student's feelings and attitudes. The teacher might be so driven to teach certain points at all costs that she might ride roughshod over the feelings of the student.

CONFLICT IN THE TEACHER BETWEEN HER CONCERN FOR AN INDIVIDUAL STUDENT VS. THE WELFARE OF THE REST OF THE CLASS. This is one of the most common objections made by teachers. The teacher says, "Yes, this recommendation makes sense in terms of the individual child's needs, but how can it be done when there are thirty other children in the classroom?"

The teacher has difficulty in seeing that the other students will identify with an attitude and feeling of wanting to help one child. Their reaction will be "If she's that way with Carol, she'll be that way with me if I ever need her. If she's fair and patient with her, she'll be that way with me."

And in that large class, if the teacher understands that certain children need certain things, many times the individual assistance doesn't take a lot of time. Smaller classes, of course, allow the teacher to do more in general, but teachers should realize that if they understand the child, it doesn't take that much time for extra attention. It can be as simple as a touch on the shoulder, a comment, "You did well in the game yesterday." Some things take only a minute.

If the teacher is on the right wave length, no time will be spent needlessly in the wrong direction. Many things work in the classroom if the teacher knows what she wants to do and why.

how cope?

ANOTHER AREA OF DIFFICULTY FOR THE TEACHER CENTERS ON HER WISH TO HELP THE STUDENT VS. HER CONCERN FOR WHAT HER PRINCIPAL AND FELLOW TEACHERS WILL THINK OF HER. If the recommendation calls for a certain degree of unorthodoxy, flexibility, or permissiveness, the teacher might intellectually see the need for it, but she fears that she would be considered a poor teacher if faculty members were to walk into her room and see this kind of atmosphere. If the principal is involved in the consultation process, this will not happen. The principal will understand the teacher's approach and will also reinforce it. It is imperative to have backup support for the teacher.

An entire consultation session was devoted to a teacher's concern for a third grade boy who would masturbate whenever he was anxious. The teacher was almost panic stricken. She felt "something had to be done" because the rest of the class might start to do the same thing and what would happen if a principal, parent, or another teacher walked into her room of "third grade masturbators."

The consultant explained that masturbation was this immature youngster's way of dealing with his own anxiety, and if the teacher ignored it and concentrated on the reasons for the child's anxieties and helped him, that was all that had to be done in that situation. The teacher was greatly relieved, and within a few weeks the situation ceased.

THE TEACHER HAS DIFFICULTY IN SEPARATING HER OWN NEEDS FOR ACCOMPLISHMENT FROM THE STUDENT'S NEEDS AND ASPIRATIONS. In this case the teacher has a great need to push the student to achieve and do well thereby reflecting her own capabilities. Some have called this the "Nobel prize complex." Often the great testimony to the teacher's "Nobel prize complex" is in the achievement tests at the end of the year and the number of students who make honors. This need on the part of the teacher might block consultation recommendations calling for an easing up approach rather than the compulsive driving approach.

ANOTHER OBSTACLE THAT INTERFERES WITH THE TEACHER'S COLLABORATION WITH THE STUDENTS IS HER UNAWARENESS OF THE PHENOMENON OF TRANSFERENCE. In this case the teacher unknowingly transfers unconscious feelings about a key person in her life to one of her students. For instance, a teacher might have very sympathetic and positive feelings about a brother; she unconsciously transfers these feelings to a student who needs much more firmness and discipline, and because of this transference is overly permissive and indulgent.

In a reverse situation a recommendation might indicate that the student needs much more leniency and understanding. However, the teacher might be transferring feelings that she had for one of her own children and her need for her child to achieve. Unknowingly, the teacher is transferring these feelings to the student and driving that student much more than is in his best interest. Furthermore, transference can work both ways; the student might have transference feelings toward the teacher: e.g. "she expects too much, just like my mother." This, too, can compound the problem.

ANOTHER OBSTACLE EXISTS WHEN THE TEACHER RECOGNIZES ACCOMPLISHMENT RATHER THAN EFFORT. If the teacher really has difficulty in recognizing the efforts of the student and focuses only on what he has achieved and accomplished, the student will be very quick to sense this reaction. This conflict will interfere with the recommendation that a child needs to have his self-esteem bolstered in order to encourage his motivation.

If a student has worked diligently on a project or problem for an hour and is in need of more approval, the teacher can look at it and say, "Well, this is wrong." Obviously, that's a pretty hard-nosed attitude toward what is right and what is wrong. It would have been just as easy to say, "This is a good job and shows how hard you worked at it," and then as an aside the teacher could point out some of the errors.

And then there's the shy, quiet child whose self-concept might be enhanced if she were in the class play. Often, however, the teacher chooses the self-confident, extroverted student for the part, and the child who needs this kind of expression is in the wings. How do you get the teacher to choose the shy child for the part? This raises all kinds of questions. Will she be fair or unfair? What will the other students think? How good a performance will it be? Will it reflect on her?

THE TEACHER PRESENTS TWO CONFLICTING MESSAGES TO THE

STUDENT AT THE SAME TIME. In this case it is impossible for the student to respond to both messages and please the teacher. In psychiatric jargon this is called *double bind*. As a result of the consultation, the teacher's message might be, "I want you to be creative and curious and an independent, free thinker." At the same time the teacher may indicate by her actions, not verbally, that she cannot tolerate "non-conformity, deviancy, or rocking of the boat." So the teacher sends both messages to the student simultaneously, and then the student is "damned if he does and damned if he doesn't."

THE TEACHER CONFUSES SYMPATHY AND EMPATHY. In many cases the consultation recommendation has been directed toward helping the teacher empathize with the student. Empathy means the message to the student is, "I know how hard it is for you, and I know what you are going through, and I will try to be understanding and help you." Many times, however, the teacher confuses this approach with sympathy, and the message is, "Oh, you poor thing; I feel so sorry for you." And then the student feels he is an object of pity and reacts negatively to the teacher's attitude. When the empathy message gets through to the student, it is received with "Thank God, somebody understands."

Sometimes the negative feelings or hopelessness of a student is picked up by the teacher, and the teacher feels that way toward the student and cannot really help him. The student says, "I am a failure; I am really no good," and the teacher unconsciously begins to feel, "I am a worthless teacher for you." Very often the consultant can help the teacher see that she has picked up the student's hopelessness rather than used her own assessment of any areas of strength and try to use them to help the student.

THE TEACHER IS SOMETIMES UNAWARE THAT SHE IS TREATING STUDENTS IN THE SAME MANNER AS SHE WAS TREATED AS A STUDENT. She is displacing feelings she had as a student toward certain teachers. She is unconsciously saying, "Now you are going to suffer the way I had to," although she is consciously trying to function as a teacher and not as the student of the past that is still in her.

How often have you heard a teacher or some other authority figure say, "In my day we had it much rougher, and you really had to toe the line." The unspoken message is, "Why should you be happy now and why should you have it any better. Look what I had to go through."

FOLLOWING CONSULTATION, THE TEACHER IS NOT A THERAPIST, SHE IS STILL A TEACHER. The consultation is not asking the teacher to be a co-therapist; it is asking the teacher to draw on her strength as a human being to deal with students who are fellow humans. To oversimplify this point, it's almost like the golden rule; treat others as you would like to be treated. Courtesy and manners are often neglected. Consultation helps teachers become more aware of their limitations and more willing to accept them. If teachers can accept themselves better, then they can accept their limitations and, just as important, those of their students.

Very often the cornerstone of consultation is the way in which the teacher identifies with the consultant, and this fact is corroborated by other mental health consultants. Just as the consultant sets up a model to deal with teachers, the teachers, consciously or unconsciously, might use the same model to deal with their students. The consultant who can say, "I don't know; I have limitations," or "I don't have all the answers," can enable the teacher to be that way with the student, helping to foster a freer climate. The teacher realizes that she has limits in dealing with a child without being critical of herself.

CONFLICT BETWEEN THE TRADITIONAL AND ORTHODOX VS. THE LIBERAL, PROGRESSIVE, AND UNORTHODOX EDUCATIONAL PATTERNS. In some cases the teacher will have difficulty adapting to the attitudes of today's students, and educational recommendations will conflict with the traditional patterns the teacher has practiced. The teacher who is the student of the past might have trouble being the teacher of today. Open discussion with students can help here.

ANOTHER AREA OF DIFFICULTY IS THE TEACHER VS. SAVIOR (A COROLLARY TO THE TEACHER VS. THERAPIST). Often the teacher leaves the consultation session with renewed hope and conviction and sallies forth "to save this youngster," forgetting the limitations of the classroom, the student, and herself. This might cause unnecessary complications and disappointment. This can escalate as the "more the student is drowning, the more the teacher tries to save him."

THE SHOULDS VS. THE COULDS. No matter how much the consultation points out that the teacher should approach a student on the level at which he *can* function, the teacher has a preconceived idea of the level at which the student *should* function. It is very difficult for her to approach the student based on what he can do, because the idea of what he should be doing interferes and blocks. Just as she expects more from the student, she expects more from herself, without accepting what can really be taught and learned in this situation. If the consultant is aware of this fact, he will try to help the teacher to expect less of herself. If this is accomplished, the teacher can then judge the child more accurately.

THE TEACHER IS THREATENED BY CLOSENESS TO THE STUDENT, PREFERRING TO KEEP A CERTAIN DEGREE OF DISTANCE. Sometimes the consultation calls for more involvement with a particular student. If this is threatening, the teacher will find it very difficult although she might go through the motions of more involvement. Sometimes a teacher says, "I don't want to know too much about a student because it will bother me. The less you know, the better off you are." This is especially true of youngsters from troubled homes. It might make the teacher feel more guilty.

POWER STRUGGLE IN THE AREA OF THE CHILD'S FAILURE RATHER THAN IN HIS SUCCESS. A teacher locks horns with a student who fails to do a book report, and the power struggle is centered on the child's failure rather than working together toward success. It's a battle in the negative area.

What if the child has had no successes? It's up to the teacher to set up an arena where the child can have success. If a problem centers on book reports, giving him more book reports isn't the answer because it reinforces his failure. He's demonstrated an inability to comply, and there's no point in giving him more opportunities to fail. The teacher is encouraged to look at the area of potential strength or success and try to reinforce that aspect. "Okay, you can't do a book report. Is there a poster you'd like to make based on the theme of the book you read?" It is surprising, but often the power struggle obscures any positive reinforcement.

ANOTHER AREA OF POWER STRUGGLE IS TO CONTROL OR BE

CONTROLLED. In this situation the teacher sees her relationship or interaction with the student as a power struggle for control rather than as a collaborative one. Therefore, the teacher feels that she must be very firm and in control at all times; otherwise, "the students will be in control and there will be utter chaos and no learning."

Effective application of recommendations made in consultation often will be hindered by these obstacles. Often it is necessary to have brief follow-through meetings with the consultees. These meetings not only will maintain the consultant-consultee relationship in an on-going way, but consultees can get help if obstacles are interfering with the optimal application of recommendations from the consultation session.

Follow-through can take place at the next consultation session, although it can be effective in the hallway or in the classroom. It can be as simple as "How is Johnny doing . . . ?"

CHAPTER 8

CONSULTATION WITH OTHER GROUPS OF SCHOOL PERSONNEL

Thus far we have focused primarily on school consultation with teachers principally because it is the most frequent type of consultation in schools. It is important to note, however, that many of the approaches used in the consultation process with teachers can also apply to other groups of school personnel. Each group has its own characteristics, and this chapter will deal with consultation with other school personnel including school administrators and pupil personnel workers.

As already stated, the aim of consultation is to help the learning child, and to be effective, almost any form of consultation has to involve the teachers directly or indirectly. Many times, however, consultation with teachers is not feasible in the school system, and the consultant has to start consultation with other groups of school personnel.

CONSULTATION WITH SCHOOL ADMINISTRATORS

The importance of getting the support of school administrators has been emphasized earlier. Without the administrator's cooperation, very little can take place in terms of effective consultation with his faculty in his school district.

In addition, at times it can be very helpful to have the administrators as one of the primary consultation groups. This group can include the school superintendent, his assistant, principals, or any other key administrators. This type of consultation involves the unique concerns and how the consultant can address himself and be of help with the concerns shared in common by the administrators.

How do you get administrators to realize the need for the

process · divorced
from content

consultant's services? At first most administrators feel little need of consultant services, and very rarely have they permitted themselves to work in a consultant-consultee relationship at the beginning of a school consultation program. They will give the consultant some time and support in many cases, and they will issue the go-ahead signal and perhaps delegate an assistant to work with the consultant. It's only later on that they may begin to get involved. If they become less threatened by the consultant and feel that this outsider is trying to help, they sometimes begin to feel that they would like to have some of this help for themselves.

Administrators often begin to see the need for consultation when the consultant starts to have an impact on the school faculty. Since the administrators feel they have to be in control of what is happening in the school district, sooner or later the administrator, on his own initiative, may want to get involved as a means of becoming more informed as well as in control of what is happening. He wants to feel that he still has his finger on the pulse of the system. Thus, successful consultation within the ranks may create ripples that will stir most administrators to get more involved, although in the beginning the administrators are too busy, and the new program does not have a high enough priority.

At all times administrators are concerned about balancing the service needs of the district against preventive types of consultation such as in-service training and modifying teacher attitudes. This is particularly true when the school administrator is always concerned about adverse notoriety if a particular crisis gets publicity or is not handled well.

Some administrators are very crisis-oriented and want to be involved in crisis situations only. Their motivation toward any kind of preventive consultation is limited. In other cases, the administrator has certain personal axes to grind and hopes consultation will help with these problems. In a previous chapter, an example was cited of the administrator who was being pressured by the school board to work on his teachers who were too punitive and used too much corporal punishment. The administrator's main purpose in consultation was to get the consultant to modify the teachers' behavior.

What are the main problems that motivate administrators to seek consultation help? First, the school administrator is expected to carry out the mandate of the school board which reflects feelings and pressures of the community, and at the same time in his role as a professional educator, he wants to provide a quality education for as many children as possible. This is the major conflict situation faced by administrators, and almost every administrator has voiced this concern in consultation—some with minor concern, others with major anxiety.

Specifically, this conflict centers on such issues as trying to provide quality education which often requires a large budget, pressure to meet teacher demands, and need for specialized curriculum and programs, while at the same time trying not to aggravate the citizens of the community who are already up in arms about high taxes. The school administrator constantly walks a tightrope between these two conflicting pressures.

Secondly, anxiety also is created when the community is pressuring the school administrator to do more about areas of social concern such as the dress code, sex education, the drug problem, and student discipline, and at the same time he is asked to create a climate in the school system that promotes a freer feeling and an atmosphere more conducive to learning. In other words, the school board is demanding the administrator be more suppressive and oppressive, while the need of the students and teachers is for more freedom and flexibility.

A third area of pressure centers on the old guard or traditional view toward teaching held by many citizens and school boards in conflict with the administrator's knowledge as a professional of many innovative methods to enhance education and meet the needs of today's student. Sometimes, however, the opposite occurs. The administrator can find himself in a fairly progressive community in which the school board and citizens are more of the new guard variety and want open classrooms, individualized instruction, or specialized curriculum, and the administrator finds himself dealing with a faculty that is more traditional and orthodox in their approach.

Still another area of conflict for the school administrator is the need to play politics in order to maintain his job, but at the same time he is expected to act like a true professional educator. Often the two do not mix well. Furthermore, many school administrators are placed in the bind of doing what is most feasible and expedient, and at times these actions can be at the expense of the type of personnel or programs instituted.

For instance, the school board might decide that there is a need for some form of social work in the school system, and the administrator is pressured to hire someone. If he yields to pressure, he might end up with a person who is qualified as a home and school visitor and not as a graduate social worker. Given more money and more time he could seek a well-qualified social worker.

In many ways administrators find that they are asked to maintain the status quo and not rock the boat. Yet this demand is often counter to what they as educators know will permit change and innovation. How can the administrator effect both?

Essentially these are some of the main problems facing school administrators. How then does the consultant, who finds these problems repeatedly put on the table, deal with them and be of help to the administrator?

Ways the Consultant Can be of Help to Administrators

One of the key points here is that the mental health consultant, who is child-oriented and focuses on the interaction between the school, teacher and student, is in an excellent position to serve as spokesman for the child-oriented group, and at the same time he is aware of the problems of the administrators who are more program and school-oriented. In other words, he can be a liaison, using his training and experience to form a bridge between the two.

The most important role the consultant can play in consultation with the administrator is to continually try to keep the focus on the learning child. This is his *raison d'etre* as a consultant with administrators.

If, on one hand, the consultant simply echoes the demands of the community and the school board, he is just reinforcing one side of the conflict faced by the administrator. And if he is only interested in education and does not take into account the realities faced by the administrator, he will be of very little help to the administrator.

Although the consultant is a spokesman for the student and the teacher, he has to realize that, at best, he can offer models for optimum learning, but then he must leave it up to the individual administrator to see how well the model fits his own situation and how well he can realistically make use of it. The consultant who tries to force his ideas on the administrator will create one of two reactions. He will be seen as still another pressure added to the many, or he will tend to make the administrator feel more inadequate and will be of very little help in a positive manner.

It's really not necessary for the consultant to be familiar with school programs such as open classrooms and ungraded systems. Naturally, the more the consultant knows, the more helpful it is, but if the consultant is really functioning as a liaison between the child's needs and the teacher's concerns, and as a liaison between this group and the administrator, then what the consultant has to know will come from the child and the teacher. In other words, they will tell the consultant their problems and needs and will give him some suggestions as to what will help. As the liaison, what the consultant basically has to know will come from his experience and contact with them. The consultant states the child's needs, and then these needs are fitted by the school into whatever pattern they have or can establish. The consultant does not impose his ideas; he let's them know what might be needed and lets the school take over from there.

The most important benefit of working with administrators is that this type of consultation has far reaching effects. The administrator has more power and can enable a lot of things to take place. In working with administrators, the consultant has a chance to have an impact on the entire school system rather than on just a group of teachers and their classrooms. (However, the consultant still needs contacts with teachers.)

In a particular consultation session, the superintendent was concerned with the low morale of the teachers who resisted any kind of change requiring adjustment or more work. His main interest in the consultation was to get the morale and attitude of the teachers on a more professional level. The consultant found the basic problem was very poor communication between the administrator and his faculty. The administrator viewed this as low morale and poor attitude on the part of the teachers, but the teachers looked at the administrator as an educator in an ivory tower who really could not tune in on their level. The consultant assessed the situation, then used his consultant skills to encourage and support the administrator to open up channels of communication with his teachers. Specifically, the consultant agreed to work in several workshops with the teachers provided that the administrator was there and involved in the workshops. This approach provided the vehicle for the faculty and administrator to really begin to have an exchange. This type of exchange was difficult at first for the administrator, but in this way, aided by the support and guidance of the consultant, the administrator was able to later carry on in a better way. In addition, he also set up a grievance committee that could always go to him. In other words, certain things were built in as ways of trying to keep this exchange going, even after the consultant pulled out.

CONSULTATION WITH SCHOOL PRINCIPALS

Principals, like superintendents, seem to share some of the same concerns of the administrator in an educational system. However, because the principal is closer to the students and teachers, several unique aspects of consultation with school principals become apparent. There are several areas of binds and conflicts that the principal finds himself in, by nature of his job, and these create considerable anxiety in the principal. These conflicts and dilemmas for the principal are very important to be aware of, for the consultant's main function is to try to deal with the concerns, anxieties, and frustrations that they produce.

School System Orientation vs. Student Orientation. To achieve a balance between the demands of running a school program and the concern about students is the major conflict encountered by the principal: Is the school there to serve the learning child or is the student there to maintain the educational system? This problem plagues many principals especially as they become more aware of this conflict.

CONTROL OR BE CONTROLLED? A corollary to the above is the conflict of to control or to be controlled. Where does the principal draw the line? Principals are constantly struggling with this problem. If they are too liberal and flexible, then they fear loss of control over the students, faculty, and buildings. On the other hand, if they are too controlling, they often lose the trust and rapport of the faculty and students. If the principal presents an authoritarian attitude, that he is the boss of the school and the teachers are his subordinates, he is going to have a harder job than if he views himself and the teachers as co-professionals, each with his own job, responsibilities and contributions. If, however, the principal goes in the other direction and tries to be one of the gang, then he abrogates the responsibilities and contributions he can make as a principal. Some principals have that problem and then the teachers run the school according to their own needs. Conversely, if the principal is the overly stern father figure of the school, then he runs the school according to his own needs.

Since the principal very often sets the entire tone and climate of the school, one can see how invaluable the consultant might be in this particular area toward improving the overall school climate that would affect both faculty and students.

MASTER TEACHER VS. SUPERVISOR OF TEACHERS. Many principals feel their present positions are in some way the result of recognition of their success as master teachers. However, they now find themselves in the role of supervisors and administrators, and in many ways they are not prepared or trained for this position. To top that off, the job is often incompatible and in conflict with their own views and feelings as teachers. In many schools principals are asked, as former master teachers, to encourage and help the faculty. However, at the same time they are asked to supervise and write rating reports on these same teachers. It is a rare teacher who can bare her inadequacies to her principal when that very same principal is going to rate her. The principal, in a sense, finds himself trying to wear two hats: master teacher and administrator-supervisor.

The consultant will find that certain peculiarities will begin to emerge in this type of group consultation. Many times principals will speak of teachers as "those teachers" in exactly the same way teachers speak of students as "those kids" when there is a problem. And just as with the teacher and the student, the consultant at all times tries to foster a more collaborative relationship between the principal and the faculty.

TEACHER ADVOCATE VS. CHILD ADVOCATE. When the teacher sends a student to the principal's office because she can't handle the child in the classroom, she is automatically assuming that the principal has certain skills to help the child that she herself doesn't possess. Often this is expected by dint of the authority of the principal's office. The teacher looks to the principal to take over where she has failed, yet in many ways, the principal has no more qualifications than the teacher to handle the child more successfully. The rationale here is that the teacher has the child in class everyday and she can't solve the problem. What makes her think the principal can when he has much less of a relationship with the student? The consultant can help here by enabling the principal to accept this realization about himself, to share this with the teacher, and then (this is the collaborative part), see what ways *they* can help the student. If this can be accomplished, there is more chance of success. Principals repeatedly express the same concerns. On the secondary level, the problem is to get teachers to feel more student-oriented. As one principal aptly stated, "I have some teachers who say, 'I teach math,' and others who say, 'I teach kids, and math.' " Some are more child-oriented and others are more subject-oriented. Principals often mention that many times they feel they're caught in the middle of conflicts between students and teachers, and many times they are not sure how to handle the situation without taking sides. In addition, there is the problem of discipline. Teachers feel they are supposed to have uniform measures for various kinds of disciplinary problems, yet this can be in conflict at times when it is felt that individual disciplinary measures are necessary. In other words, it may be expected that the principal should handle all students in the same way, yet the principal might feel that each child needs an individualized approach.

EDUCATIONAL VS. ADMINISTRATIVE NEEDS. Another concern facing principals is making optimal use of their personnel and at the same time, meeting administrative obligations. For example, many principals realize that guidance counselors spend too much time filling out pre-college questionnaires and doing other paper work at the expense of counseling students. Yet they find it hard to juggle the two demands.

YESTERDAY'S STUDENT VS. TODAY'S PRINCIPAL. Another area of concern that emerges in consultation with principals centers on the conflict of their own personal value system and the divergent values of some students and young teachers. This is especially true in today's society. In a sense, many principals are the students of yesterday, and those feelings and attitudes enter into their present role of working with today's students. The gap there can sometimes be quite wide.

In a specific case, the consultation was centered on student dress and length of hair. The consultant asked the principal to take a minute and look around the group. There in the group of eight principals, dress ranged from a modish principal with fairly long hair and long sideburns to another who was ultraconservative in dress. When the group recognized their individual variances, they wondered aloud about having uniform expectations of the students. The principals had a good laugh at this realization, and this action helped them to be more flexible with the students, seeing that there is no right or wrong among themselves, just a difference in personal taste in dress.

These are some of the main problems and binds that the principal has in his position in the school system. Consultation can be very helpful to principals for many of the same reasons that administrators could find consultation valuable. Through the group consultation approach, principals have an opportunity to deal with their feelings of alienation and loneliness by sharing their concerns with each other as well as offering suggestions. One of the most important functions for the consultant is to foster a climate that permits this sharing to take place. It is understandable that principals will have many of these feelings. Often, it is not always a reflection of their inadequacies, but in many cases, it is a reflection of their job. Consultation gives principals support so that they can open up to each other. In so doing, they help work out many other problems that their job creates.

Just as with administrators, the consultant can appreciate the problems facing principals, but at the same time he can try to be the spokesman for the student and teacher because of his child-orientation background and his focus on interaction between the student and the teacher or school. This serving as a spokesman for the child-teacher and as a liaison person between the principal and the students and faculty can be of considerable help in the consultation.

It should be pointed out that there is a major difference in consultation with principals of elementary schools and principals of secondary schools. In many ways, the principal of a junior or senior high school has greater concerns than does the elementary principal. Many elementary principals already have a more built-in collaborative relationship with their teachers and a more intimate knowledge of their students. This is the result of the age group of their students, the size of their school, and the self-contained classrooms. Thus, most elementary schools are more child-oriented and this creates less of the problems resulting from the gap between a program orientation versus a child orientation. At the secondary level, there is much more subject orientation and less student orientation.

The consultant will find that principals, as well as administrators, are concerned about the amount of investment made in the small number of students with the problems if the help is at the expense of the greater number of students with fewer problems. In addition, many principals feel that parents dump all their responsibilities for child rearing onto the school and then make all kinds of unreasonable demands. Yet, the same principals realize that teaching today involves more than curriculum, and here again it's the problem of finding a balance between the responsibility of the home and the responsibility of the school.

Perhaps the chief area of conflict, as voiced also by administrators, is the need to respond to the messages that students and teachers are sending out and at the same time take care of the "waves" that superintendents, school boards and parents are creating.

In view of the aforementioned situations, we may summarize the role that the consultant can provide in consultation with the principals.

First of all, by bringing principals together and acting as a catalyst in the group consultation, the consultant can help considerably with the concerns and problems that the principal has in his job. It also facilitates, through the group process, principals helping each other.

Secondly, the consultant can help as a resource person with the principals. Due to his knowledge of child development and human behavior, he can be of considerable help to the principals with child-related problems, teacher-related problems, and inter-personal problems such as communication breakdown, staff rivalries, and jealousies.

Thirdly, as a liaison person between the faculty and children and between faculty and the principal, the consultant can help facilitate the very necessary collaborative feeling that permits a school to function better and allows the principal to do a better job.

Fourth, the consultant who is not only a liaison person within the school, but also a liaison person between the school and the community, can be of help to the principal. Many outside community collaborations can be improved between the principal and these agencies (for instance, mental health facilities and child care agencies), because of the consultant's knowledge and involvement with both the school and these community facilities.

Needless to say, consultation with principals can be invaluable. As already mentioned, most consultations with teachers about students need the principal's understanding and support. Furthermore, since in many cases the principal's attitude influences the attitude of the entire school, any help in this area will benefit the entire school.

CONSULTATION WITH PUPIL PERSONNEL STAFF

Here in this type of consultation, I am talking about working with guidance counselors, nurses, home and school visitors, school social workers, and psychologists. These people are the non-teaching professionals in the school family, and in many ways their job is the same as that of the mental health consultant. They are the consultants to teachers and children from within the school system. There are some particular characteristics and problems for pupil personnel workers as non-teachers in the school system. These can be described as follows.

Conflict With Mental Health Consultant

The overlapping of roles between pupil personnel workers as internal consultants and mental health consultants as external consultants can bring with it certain difficulties. It can arouse inter-professional rivalry and its consequent negative effects. Sometimes a pupil personnel worker may feel that the consultant will take over his or her domain. Consultants sometimes don't realize that this fear exists. Therefore, it is important not to by-pass or encroach on the territory of the pupil personnel worker, but to make as much positive use of the presence of these pro-fessionals. The object of consultation should be to help the pupil personnel worker make better use of himself. Many times the pupil personnel worker can be misused and even abused by the school.

Conflict Between the Pupil Personnel Worker and Teachers

Teachers frequently use the pupil personnel worker as a dumping ground. If the student presents a problem, the teacher will say, "Go see Mr. Smith." It's the old buck passing game. The teacher often doesn't see herself as a collaborator with the pupil personnel worker. Often within the system, there isn't enough communication, and the pupil personnel worker doesn't know what is going on in class and the teacher doesn't know what's going on in the guidance counselor's office. The student then, is not getting the maximum benefit. Instead of pooling talent, there might even be direct conflict. The teacher says, "The guidance counselor is of no help; he stays in his fancy office and doesn't have to teach thirty kids." On the other hand, the guidance counselor may say, "The teacher is not really interested in the problems of individual students."

Conflict Between the Pupil Personnel Worker and Administration

Sometimes the administrator, in his concern about the school program, often misuses the guidance counselor to work in areas of vocational planning, college preparation, curriculum aspects, and other administrative matters. This takes the pupil personnel worker away from helping specific children. The guidance counselor may say, "I was trained to counsel and instead I'm an assistant administrator." It is thus important that the consultant try to help teachers and administrators to properly and effectively use the pupil personnel workers.

Among the pupil personnel workers, the main person who encounters the above problems is the guidance counselor. To a lesser extent, some of these problems are encountered by school social workers, home and school visitors, and school psychologists. The only person on the pupil personnel staff who is in a much more favorable position is the school nurse.

The school nurse has many positives in her job situation within the school system. First of all, in running a type of first aid station for children who don't feel well, they have an opportunity to see many children who are showing signs of emotional difficulties. For example, the poor math student who comes in complaining of stomachaches during his geometry class, or the nonathletic student who gets sick in gym class. Not only does the school nurse have an opportunity to see many children who are having emotional problems, but she also is able to do so in an on-going and nonthreatening way. She sometimes gets to know students better than the teacher, and because she isn't a threat, she is in a position to be more helpful. Furthermore, the nurse often gets to know the families of problem children, and thus this adds another dimension to her role in better understanding the student and being able to be more supportive. Another advantage that the school nurse has is that she is not bound to a classroom and thus has more mobility and more chance to give students some individual attention. Still another aspect of the advantageous position of the school nurse is that since she is in a medical role, she is more likely to be seen as a helping person.

In addition to the advantages that the school nurse has within the school system as just mentioned, she also has certain potentials as a liaison person not only within the school system, but also outside of it. The school nurse many times has had contacts with outside agencies and can be a knowledgeable liaison person between the school and these agencies. Therefore, any consultative help and support to the school nurse can be quite helpful for the student, for his family, and for the school itself.

CONSULTATION WITH THE PUPIL PERSONNEL TEAM

The pupil personnel team concept is a very popular one and one which I very strongly believe in. Consultation with this group has proven to be very productive and worthwhile. Before examining the many advantages of consultation with this group, it may be best to understand who the team members are. The ideal pupil personnel team consists of the pupil personnel workers [guidance counselor, nurse, social worker, psychologist], teachers of the student who is having difficulties, an administrator (the principal or his assistant), and any other specialized school personnel who may have a particular involvement such as a speech therapist. In addition to these various school personnel, at times one might want to include professionals from outside agencies that have a particular reason for being involved with the student. This might be the child's therapist, if he is receiving therapy, or a worker at the local Y who spends time with the student outside of school.

The main focus of the pupil personnel team is to have a ready resource available in the school to help with problem students. The presence of each member of the team makes a particular contribution to the team's overall effectiveness. The necessity for having the student's teachers present is quite obvious. They will be able to share with the team their daily observations of the student's strengths and weaknesses, why they are concerned, and what has been done to help the student thus far. The importance of having the teachers present is not only to shed more light on the problem, but also, since any meaningful recommendations that the team might arrive at must involve the teachers participation, their presence in the making of the decisions and recommendations is invaluable.

The presence of a school administrator on the team is also quite important. He has the power to effect change and to permit or block recommendations that the team might develop. At the same time, even though he doesn't teach the problem student, he can get intimate understanding of the child, bringing him closer to the student and the student's helpers.

The value of having pupil personnel workers as part of the team is also quite apparent. They already know a great deal about the student and his family and have a groundwork from which subsequent understanding can grow. In addition, due to their liaison work with outside agencies and families, very often they will play a significant role in the carrying out of the team's recommendations.

This then is the makeup of the team and some understanding of who is there, and why. At this point we are now better able to understand the many advantages of consultation to pupil personnel teams and reasons for its popularity.

First of all, the pupil personnel teams are already serving as the internal consultants and a ready resource within the school system. It is something like getting sick in the middle of the night and knowing you have a family doctor. If school personnel know that the pupil personnel team is on hand, it is very helpful and re-assuring in dealing with difficult problems.

Another major advantage of the pupil personnel team is that it brings together and pools the understanding of the student so that the total picture of the total child can, hopefully, be developed. Thus, we will get understanding of the child from the vantage point of classroom observations, home visits, community involvement, and in some cases, psychological testing. This pooling helps alleviate the fragmentation that is often found in large school systems.

Each member of the pupil personnel team can bring his own view of the student, thus the English teacher may have an entirely different view than the physical education teacher and either one might not have had the benefit of the other's observations. Almost all the people on the team have been involved with the student somewhere along the line and now they can come together and try to integrate what they think and observe. This can save many extra smaller meetings and is much more economical in terms of time and practicality. Furthermore, with the administrator as part of the team, he can learn what is going on, what is being recommended, and why.

Another aspect of this advantage of a team concept is that often the teacher may be relieved about her own feelings of inadequacy when she hears how other people have had problems with the student. Also, she might have the feeling that the principal thinks she is a poor teacher, but now after what he learns in the discussion, she may feel reassured that he better understands. By being part of the team, school personnel can become supportive of each other. In receiving this support, each participant sheds the feeling that he is working alone. Suddenly the teacher realizes she has the same concerns, doubts, and uncertainties as the guidance counselor.

Thus, we can see that by bringing the various team members together, another advantage of this approach becomes evident. In the process of sharing of knowledge about the child and by getting together, a team spirit can be established and this can help markedly with the frequently found rivalries, jealousies, and power struggles that might be present within the school.

Still another advantage of the team is that all the major representatives from the school who have an impact on the student's life are present. As a result of this, there can be considerable spillover from the consultations that can reach many other school personnel who would not otherwise be involved.

As we have already seen, one of the major advantages of the team concept is the pooling of the understanding of the total child. In addition to this, since the recommendations that the team will come up with will involve their being carried out in most cases by the team members, or other people that the team members are associated with, it is very helpful to have these people present in the decision-making process. In summary then, we see that the use of the pupil personnel team, as described, essentially helps in gaining a better understanding of the student, in effecting a more collaborative relationship between different intra-school disciplines, and promotes a more effective follow-through and application of consultation recommendations.

Thus far we have looked at the composition of the pupil personnel team and the advantages of this type of consultation. Very little has been said about the role of the consultant in working with pupil personnel teams.

First of all, the main purpose of a consultant, again acting as a catalyst and resource person, is to keep the focus on the child under discussion. This means fostering the participant's understanding of the child and not allowing power struggles or other obstructions to divert the reason for their working together.

Secondly, in this role, the consultant should, as much as possible, function as a leader *in* the group rather than the leader *of* the group. This is important to keep in mind since, as we have seen before, the pupil personnel team already is, in a way, the school's consultant.

Thirdly, the consultant can play a major role in fostering team spirit and collaboration by the manner in which he collaborates with the team. I have seen considerable positive identification take place by team members through the manner in which the consultant collaborated with them.

The fourth function of the consultant is to act as a resource person who, as much as possible, will try and provide professional input without promoting undue dependency upon himself. Many times, if the consultant handles himself in a manner that helps bring his understanding to the situation and promotes a kind of in-service training, the team members will grow in their own development and not just get answers to problem children. This can lead to the point that the consultant will not be needed to attend every pupil personnel meeting and only be asked to attend when the team members feel they cannot handle the situation themselves.

The value of consultation through pupil personnel teams has been repeatedly demonstrated. In one school district, where the teachers were striking and negotiating for professional development, they asked for the consultant to work with their pupil personnel team. They had such services with positive results and felt very strongly about continuing this. It had not only helped them with disturbed children, but also had enhanced their own professional development. In another situation where I directed a three-year federally funded demonstration consultation project, it was interesting to note what happened after the project was completed. Now that any further consultation would have to be paid for by the school districts themselves, a weeding took place, and the districts decided to keep certain aspects of the consultation project that they felt were most valuable and also, realistically, most economical. The one that they almost universally chose to fund and continue was the pupil personnel team meetings with the hiring of a consultant to continue lending his support to them. In other districts that had used and favored the pupil personnel team consultation model, when they no longer were provided with mental health consultation by the school system, they turned to the local community mental health centers to provide them with a consultant.

CHAPTER *9*

DIVERSE OUTGROWTHS
OF CONSULTATION

Aꜱᴛʜᴏᴜɢʜ ᴛʜᴇ ᴘʀɪᴍᴀʀʏ ɢᴏᴀʟ of mental health consultation in the schools is to help the learning child, many by-products can result from the consultation process itself. Some of these offshoots can be anticipated as extensions of the consultations. However, some are unexpected, surprising, but yet meaningful. It is important for school administrators to know what can result from consultation in the school system.

The best way to approach these spinoffs is to go back to the public health model outlined in Chapter 5 where primary, secondary, and tertiary prevention were considered. To recap, primary prevention is mainly programs for a healthy student population to prevent any learning or emotional problems. Secondary prevention is early diagnosis and therapeutic intervention of now existent problems. Tertiary prevention deals with rehabilitation of chronic, long-standing problems.

Within this framework, let's look at some programs. Certain prerequisites have to be established, however, before by-products can take place.

Cᴏʟʟᴀʙᴏʀᴀᴛɪᴏɴ. School personnel must have an attitude that learning is a collaboration between the student and the teacher and that education is a collaborative process.

Bɪʟᴀᴛᴇʀᴀʟ Aᴅᴀᴘᴛᴀᴛɪᴏɴ. There has to be an attitude of mutual adaptation on the part of the school as well as on the part of the students for most programs to succeed. + consultant

Aᴄᴛɪᴠᴇ Iɴᴠᴏʟᴠᴇᴍᴇɴᴛ. Again, any successful consultation program has to have the active involvement of school personnel. Often this may be the teacher or the principal, but it must be someone in the school system who is actually involved in the program and not merely a passive spectator.

A Fᴏᴄᴜꜱ ᴏɴ Uɴᴅᴇʀʟʏɪɴɢ Cᴀᴜꜱᴇꜱ. Wherever possible, the consultation program should not be aimed simply at the change of symptoms or behavior. It should try to deal with some of the underlying causes. This objective will contribute much to the success of the consultation program.

With these prerequisites in mind, let's take a look at some consultation programs at the various levels of prevention.

AT THE PRIMARY PREVENTION LEVEL

A YEAR WITH EIGHT PRINCIPALS. In consultation with eight high school principals during a school year, one concern became increasingly clear: There is a need for more time for teachers to spend with students who have special needs whether in the academic area or in guidance counseling. The principals realized there was very little free time during the rigid school day (seven or eight periods) , and the busing schedule did not allow teachers to be available to students after school.

At the end of the year of consultation, one of the principals decided that he would introduce an optional period the following year, setting aside one period during the school day for students to go to any teacher for any reason. Teachers would remain in their classrooms and be available to students. If a student had a particular concern, maybe math, he could go to that teacher for some tutoring. If there was a crisis in a personal or home situation, and the student had a very good relationship with the teacher, the optional period would give the student a chance to talk with the teacher. Interestingly enough, teachers who did not have good relationships with students found themselves in empty classrooms with no students. The empty classrooms served as a catalyst to help some teachers examine their relationship to students, and this led to some attitude change on the part of these teachers.

Students were told that they were free to use the optional period in any way that they felt would benefit them. The only restriction was to stay in the school building. Study hall or an activity such as basketball were options too. This free time built into the school day became a highly successful feature at the high school, and although this program took place in a very new and costly school, students noted that of all the innovations in the school, the optional period was their favorite one.

This change was a direct outgrowth of consultation with principals, and the learning atmosphere in the entire high school was enhanced. Previously, the desire for better collaboration between students and teachers might have been there, but it was not physically possible because of the way the school day was structured. The change would not have taken place if the principal had not been involved in the consultation group and on his own had come to see the need for it.

A THREE-MONTH EXPERIMENT. Another example of the extension of consultation on the primary prevention level involved a first grade teacher who was in a consultation group. The teacher, who had many years of experience, found that more than half of her students were slow readers and were not progressing according to the usual reading methods. She also felt they were immature and "not ready."

Through support of consultation, and with the cooperation of her principal, she was permitted to discontinue all formal teaching of reading and turned her attention to helping the youngsters relax more in class with play and game activities focusing on motor skills. She did this for almost three months, and then felt that the students were ready for the more formal aspects of reading. The result was that almost all the learning to read was done in the last three months of school, and almost every child learned to read well enough to go on to the second grade level of reading.

The teacher pointed out that without support of consultation she never would have dared to follow this approach. Yet from past experience she felt that many of the children would not have learned to read well enough to go on to the second grade if she had followed the more formal and traditional approach.

PRESCHOOL SCREENING PROGRAM. Another school district recognized that many children in school had some type of learning handicap, either perceptual motor or just immaturity. Often by the time they were identified, sometime during kindergarten, they were not ready for first grade, and in a sense were already a potential failure. Through consultation, a preschool screening program was developed in which four-year-old children who were being registered for kindergarten also were evaluated at the same time. The consultant and kindergarten teacher observed the children in a play group in the kindergarten room and also conducted a separate interview with each child. At the same time a pupil personnel worker interviewed the mother. As a result of the screening, children in need of extra help and support to prepare them for kindergarten and school were enrolled in a new preschool program to give them an extra year of help before entering school. The program included more social interaction, more group play, and development of motor skills.

TAKE ME TO YOUR MAGIC CIRCLE. Consultation in another school pointed up the need for teachers and students to have more opportunity to work in the affective sphere of learning; namely, feelings and attitudes about themselves, the school, and their peers. As a result of consultation in several elementary schools, consultation led to the development of a program along the lines of the Magic Circle. Three times a week for about a half hour, teachers and students sat in a circle talking about various personal feelings. As a result, many of the apprehensions, fears, and blocks to a freer learning climate were reduced.

ESTABLISHING OPEN CLASSROOMS. As a result of consultation in several schools, it was felt that there was a need for a freer classroom climate, and one that would allow more variations to meet the needs of individual students. This led to establishing of several open classrooms with the support of the consultant. After the consultation had been discontinued, the open classrooms remained as an integral part of those schools.

AT THE SECONDARY PREVENTION LEVEL

FORMATION OF PUPIL PERSONNEL TEAMS. The most obvious by-product at this level occurred in the formation of the pupil personnel teams. Not only did the involvement of a consultant help in the formation of these teams, but as a result, the teams' impact often extended to many others in the school including other teachers, administrators, and specialized school personnel. This allowed the development, through the team operation, of early diagnosis and remediation.

GROUP WORK WITH STUDENTS BY SCHOOL PERSONNEL. In a number of cases, teachers in consultation groups began to realize the importance of mutual respect and better working relationships with students. As a result of this, they organized groups of students around specific problem areas that they would work with. Thus, some teachers formed regularly scheduled discussion groups with students who were underachievers. A nurse chose to work with a group of obese teenage girls. Some other teachers chose to work with students who seemed to be overly passive, shy, and withdrawn. Still other teachers selected students who seemed extremely aggressive and hostile.

In each case the teachers became involved voluntarily in these groups as a result of their consultation experience. In some of these teacher-student groups, the consultant went beyond his role as a consultant to the teacher group. He also functioned as a consultant to the teacher in her actual group work with the students, and this type of backup consultation helped the teacher to feel more confident in this non-teaching role.

Still another example of group work by school personnel was an experience with guidance counselors. In this particular situation, guidance counselors from nine suburban school districts assembled together to make use of the opportunity of having a psychiatric consultant one afternoon a week and a social worker one day per week. They decided that the best use of the limited time of the mental health consultants would be to get consultation in doing small group counseling. This idea took hold and as time progressed, the guidance counselors began to work with groups of children in their various school districts.

From this teachers became interested and some also began to get involved in working with groups of problem students. What then unfolded was that the initial consultation was by the mental health consultants to the guidance counselors and then, as time progressed and the guidance counselors became more knowledgeable, they became the consultants to the teachers. As a result of this, approximately 1,500 students were involved in small groups in a four-year period. In all probability, very few of these students would have received any help at all. Changes took place in the students as well as the teachers and guidance counselors. This is a good example of optimal use of professional consultation time in a most economical fashion.

THE SCHOOL CUSTODIAN AS CONSULTEE. Another example of an extension of consultation occurred in an elementary school in a socially disadvantaged neighborhood. Many of the female teachers and principal felt that some of the younger boys needed a strong male identity figure. Many of the children came from fatherless homes, and almost all of the teachers in the school were female. It happened that the school custodian was a very good father figure and already had established positive relationships on his own with many of the boys. Once this fact was recognized, the custodian was invited to join the consultee group, and attention was given to his attitudes and abilities that helped him to work better with students with special problems. This might sound unorthodox, but it is an illustration of an unexpected extension of the more formal consultation structure.

USE OF THE CRISIS TEACHER. In other school systems the development of the crisis teacher was a by-product of a consultation process. Consultees expressed the need for someone to help at the time of crisis or to relieve the classroom teacher if she needed to work with a student in a special situation. The crisis teacher approach, first started in Michigan, was encouraged through consultation. Since the principal was part of a consultee group, he was able to appreciate the need for this and was very helpful and supportive in establishing the crisis teacher in his school.

ESTABLISHING RESOURCE ROOMS. A similar type of situation developed in other cases where consultees felt that students at times needed a place to retreat when they had a particular difficulty. This was in place of being removed from the classroom in a humiliating fashion to stand in the hall, go to the principal's office, or be suspended. The consultees felt that the students needed a more constructive environment in which they would have a chance to pull themselves together. To meet this need, resource rooms were established to give students an opportunity to do something to help themselves feel better whether it was playing the piano, listening to music, reading, or doing schoolwork. Resource rooms were the result of consultation with principals and teachers who recognized the value of this approach rather than the customary discipline methods. It also was handled in a more confident manner because the consultees knew they had the support of the consultant.

In summary, it could be said that as consultation continued in a school system, consultees more and more began to realize the need for other supportive measures in addition to those permitted under the normal school policy. Such things as resource rooms, crisis teachers, and pupil personnel teams are all innovations to help the school to adapt better to some of the special needs of students. Consultation reinforces the need for these supportive measures and helps to get these measures put into action.

AT THE TERTIARY PREVENTION LEVEL

MORE PROFESSIONAL REFERRALS TO LOCAL AGENCIES. At the tertiary level of prevention, several examples can be cited. One of the most helpful is the facilitation of the referral process for students with severe problems to local agencies. Often in the past students were simply identified as having problems and referred to outside agencies such as a mental health clinic or family and children's service.

As a result of consultation, school personnel became more involved in the referral process itself. Now it was the person who had the best relationship with that student who often was the one to facilitate the referral process. Thus, it could be anyone from the teacher, principal, guidance counselor, to school social worker. This person would not only help the student and parents to be prepared for the referral but would also be involved in further follow-through.

Thus, the sharing of information about the family and child with the agency was more meaningful. Many agencies noted the difference in the quality of the referrals from schools where there was a consultation program in the school, in contrast to where there wasn't any. They remarked that "the referrals were better and the agency was being used appropriately and not as a dumping ground; that students and parents were better prepared as to what to expect from the agency and its services; and that the whole climate of the referral was on a more positive note." Thus, as a result of consultation, the stage was set for more effective collaboration between clinic and school and more effective follow-through on the school's part subsequently.

ESTABLISHMENT OF CLASSES FOR THE SOCIALLY AND EMOTION-

ALLY MALADJUSTED. Setting up of special classes for emotionally and socially maladjusted children is still another example of the extension of consultation at the tertiary prevention level. In these classes children with serious learning difficulties produced by emotional problems are provided with a place in which they can cope with the educational program. Often these classes have been an outgrowth of consultation where the consultee identifies these students and the mental health consultant helped to evaluate them and together they arrived at this placement. In addition, the consultant then has been of help in providing ongoing consultation to the teacher and aide once these classes have been established.

PROPER PLACEMENT FOR SERIOUSLY DISTURBED STUDENTS. An extension of consultation can be the necessary placement of seriously disturbed students in residential treatment centers or psychiatric facilities. In many of these cases, the student has been the nemesis of the school due to his emotional disturbance (bizarre behavior, fire-setting, or vandalism) and all that has been done is to valiantly try to maintain the student in school. An extension of the consultation has been to properly identify these students and to get them the kind of help that is indicated outside of the school system.

PROPER REINTEGRATION OF THE SICK STUDENT BACK INTO THE SCHOOL SYSTEM. Conversely, consultation can also work the other way. As an extension of the process, the consultant helps the student who has already been hospitalized to return to school. This has involved working with school personnel, giving them insight into the student's problems, and encouragement and support to the faculty to create a favorable reception for the student's return. An example of this type of intervention has already been described.

CONSULTATION AS ADVISOR TO THE SCHOOL BOARD. In another instance, consultation extended to the school board itself. In a case where a boy with a history of temper outbursts and aggressive behavior brought a hunting rifle to school, great anxiety was precipitated. Many parents, because of this student's notorious reputation, expressed concern to the school board and sought to have the boy expelled. The consultant learned that the student had brought his hunting rifle to school to show his teacher because this teacher was the only one who showed some positive interest in him, and both shared an interest in hunting. The teacher was using this approach as means of reaching the student. In response, the student had begun to establish good rapport with the teacher, and part of this was his bringing the rifle to school. Through consultation intervention the school board was helped to see that this was actually a positive situation rather than a negative or unfavorable one. It was the first "reaching out" attempt by the student. When this information was shared with the school board by the consultant and their anxiety alleviated, the board was able to permit this action rather than act in a punitive manner. From this episode, the school board began to see more potential value of working with the consultant and this led to regular sessions with the consultant where they later got into school board policy, hiring of personnel, and questions as to how to work better with parents.

In conclusion, we see that whereas the consultation itself is a collaborative process, there can be many outgrowths from the consultation that can become an integral part of the school system long after the consultant has left. Furthermore, we see that these by-products can be at any level of the educational range from preschool to senior high school and at any level of prevention.

This primer may best be concluded with the words of a school board member who recently said:

> Accountability is the key word in the vocabulary of today's educators. Child advocacy is the key phrase in the language of the mental health professionals. It seems to me that we are both saying the same thing about the same kids. I think that school mental health consultation is a very good way of doing something about it.